A Teen's Life

A candid look at teens' lives through their day to day struggles.

Author

Uchenna L Umeh, MD, MBA, FAAP

Dr. Lulu aka The Momatrician

In 2012, the World Health Organization (WHO)

declared teen suicide

"a global crisis."

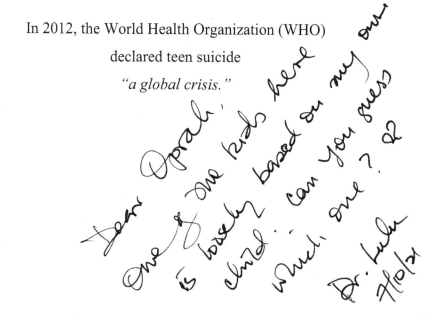

First Edition

A Teen's Life by Uchenna L. Umeh, MD, MBA, FAAP
AKA Dr. Lulu the Momatrician
by Dr. Lulu®
11844 Bandera Rd, #723 Helotes TX 78023
www.TeenAlive.com/Books

Cover by Sambriat (Fiverr.com)

ISBN: 978-1-733751-22-3

Disclaimer

This is a work of fiction. Names, characters, places and incidents either are products of the author's imagination or are used fictitiously. Any resemblance to actual persons living or dead, businesses, companies, events, or locales is entirely coincidental.

The purpose of this book is to promote broad consumer understanding and knowledge of suicide and its common causes. It is not intended to be a substitute for professional medical advice, diagnosis or treatment. Always seek the advice of your physician or other qualified healthcare provider with any questions you may have regarding medical or mental health issues. Never disregard professional medical advice or delay in seeking it because of something you read in this book.

Other Books by Uchenna L. Umeh

How to Raise Well Rounded Children

Books in the works from the How-To Series:

Bullying and Your Child 101
Your Child, Their Siblings and Mental Illness
Intentional Parenting 101
Toddlers, Tablets, Teenagers and Telephones
Teen Wellness: Your Teenager and Their Health

"This piece of information is critical, because it is contrary to what the big pharmaceutical companies would want us to believe. They push mental illness (especially depression) forward, every chance they can get. But truly, no dose or class of antidepressants can treat systematic racism. Antidepressants cannot fix a bully situation in school, nor the psychological effects of a divorce or financial crisis. Au contraire, in the past few years, prescription antidepressant use has nearly quadrupled in the United States. If indeed they are effective in treating depression as the main cause of suicidal behavior, then how do we explain the continuous and steady rise in suicide rates across all ages?"

~ Dr. Lulu®

PRAISE FOR A TEEN'S LIFE

"I like your format with the letters. It is unique. I like that you responded on a personal and professional way. It's something I have not seen before, hopefully others will enjoy that too."

~ B. Rubel

"Wonderfully and well-articulated piece of work! The book is very much needed and some parts of it made me cry... A lot! I see another 5 Star rating for you on this one Dr. Lulu!"

~ Elizabeth U

"A really great read. This work would serve any college student well as a resource. What do you think about an international annual teen or YA cross-cultural summit for those who also experienced dark moments as teens? It would be an opportunity for them to share their stories and promote awareness and hope. Sort of like a Ted Talk, but an Ask Doctor Lulu instead. It would give them a look at the weight that many others bear, as well as an opportunity for some self-reflection. I certainly had many as I was reading the letters...And I had some tearful moments too."

~ Kristy C

ACKNOWLEDGEMENTS

While writing this second book, I came to the realization that indeed a book is like a child, and the author is like a parent. One has to go through all the emotions of an expectant parent with all the trimmings, and I am proud to say this child was definitely worth every ounce of the labor pains!

I also finally internalized my quote that *"the journey of a thousand miles begins not with the first step, but with an idea!"*

The idea to write this book was conceived out of my personal need to make sense of the fact that in recent times, many-a-teenager and young adult are choosing death by their own hands, to life.

In order to fulfil that need, I had to have a plan, steady steps, and a strong support system to help me along the way, they include:

*My most loving immediate family, aka Team Uche! A gurl could never have asked for a more accommodating set of humans to ride or die with… I love y'all like *kilode!*

*My extended family, aka my never-tiring cheerleaders. All I can say is, you have known me from way back, and nothing I do should amaze you. Yet I feel like with every new chapter, you remain constant in your amazement, pride, support and love. No wonder I am fearless and blazing trails like life is a bowl of delicious jollof rice and plantains ☺

*My patients, you will forever remain my source of inspiration, and the reason I do what I do both at home and abroad. Nothing better than a group of teens to challenge you and remind you that you too were once a teenager, and that their needs today, are the exact same needs that you had yourself, once upon your teenage years.

*My Beta readers, though a small intimate group, you were *fantafreakinstic!* Correcting my grammar, suggesting alternative narratives and fixing spelling mistakes in the kindest gentlest manner.

*My friends and oh so strong support structures. You know yourselves. As I have gotten older, I have realized that less is indeed more, and quality far supersedes quantity when it comes to friends. And for that I remain eternally grateful.

*My crowd source team on Facebook. I beckoned and you responded to my requests for this and for that! May the universe guide your steps as you have wholeheartedly guided mine without holding back.

*Finally, my readers… You come last, because you are the anchor leg! You make it all worth it, for, what is a good book or even a great author without a reader?

Thank you! Thank you!! Thank you!!!

Here's to you!

Enjoy!

This work is dedicated to all those we have lost to the cruel hands

of suicide.

May you feel no more pain.

Dr. Lulu®

"I Believe it, so I can BE it"

"I believed it, so I am it"

~ Dr. Lulu®

About This Book

The crux of this book is the collection of letters written to me by 12 fictional teens from all over the world who are chronicling their struggles with life. We follow them along their individual journeys and watch as their stories unfold. We learn about their trials and tribulations, learn how they each try to juggle life's curve balls. Like us, some of their decisions are less than perfect, and may even be deadly. After each letter, I respond with advice from a physician, a mother and an empath's perspective. I then follow that with a discussion that gives an up to date information about their various situations.

I invite you to come along with them non-judgmentally, with the realization that any of these children could be yours, your family member or you. Let's look at the world through their eyes. I hope their stories open your hearts and minds to the pain and struggles of today's youth. You will discover why each of them feels alone *and* lonely in the world. Why troubled teens feel invisible, unloved, unappreciated and sometimes completely unwanted. These feelings fuel their dilemmas and influence their decisions. Each teen is lost in their unique world of darkness and despair. Each traveling a different road but ending up at the same destination, inflicting some form of self-harm as a way of coping.

My hope is that as you learn about these teens and their plights, you come away enriched, with a firm resolve to make a difference and change your outlook on certain teen behavior patterns, their causes and consequences. I also want to use this book to further my work on creating awareness for teen suicide and teen depression and their overall health and wellbeing, both mentally and emotionally. I hope to also expose some larger scale institutional wrongs that are producing the deadly ripple effect of systematic oppression and consequential emotional damage to the most innocent and most vulnerable of our planet, our children.

Let us read their stories and hopefully empathize with them. If you are a teen reading this, and you happen to see yourself or your story in here, try to give yourself permission to learn from it. If you are a parent, and experiencing conflicts with your teen, I hope that this book will help you change your attitude towards them, by seeing the world as they see it, so you can begin to be more intentional and mindful in your parenting. Indeed, most teens want one basic thing from their parents, *validation*. Some call it acceptance, some call it respect, a few call it understanding, but most of us simply call it love. Let us all start to reconnect with ourselves and each other, we are worth it, our lives are worth it, humanity is worth it. Teens, I want you to know that you are important, you are loved, you matter, your thoughts and actions matter, and most importantly, the world needs you to help light the spark that will start the change. Go forth and break the silence!

Dr. Lulu®

Table of Contents

FOREWORD

Do you ever imagine how different your life would be if you met one particular person?

I can't fathom how different my life would have been if I had met someone like Dr. Lulu when I was a teenager. What if my doctors had talked with me, not at me? What if doctors had *spent time* with me, not diagnosing, and labeling me within minutes? What if doctors' appointments lasted until the patient felt complete, not cramming a new patient into every fifteen-minute slot?

I've had the pleasure of meeting and having some dark, and funny, conversations with Dr. Lulu. She has an infectious love of life and a deep well of compassion and empathy that astounds me.

As a teenager, I attempted to kill myself — multiple times. I was a slow learner when it came to realize that I wasn't really better off dead. I was also the victim of childhood sexual abuse, but I told no one until I was 20 years old. I isolated myself and tried to numb the pain with alcohol. I ended up in rehab before I could legally drink and spent time in several mental hospitals.

If suicide has touched your life in any way, this book is for you. If addiction, trauma, or abuse has taken a toll on you or a loved one, this book is for you. We all have the right to a happy and healthy life, but sometimes we need to fight for it.

A typical book by a typical doctor might be full of so many statistics and research that your eyes glaze over after just a few pages. Luckily for us, this book and doctor are not typical. While you'll find plenty of evidence to back up the issues addressed, the real meat and benefits of this book are in the letters. While the letters are fictional, the struggles they share are not.

Dr. Lulu's practice and writings focus on at-risk children who are often ignored by society and pop culture. If you recognize yourself in any of the letters in this book, know that you are not alone. If you see a loved one in any of the following stories, know that help is available. Do take the time to give yourself the gift of healing. Don't just stop with the stories, be sure to read, and take action based on what you read in Part 3 of A Teen's Life - What to do?

Anything you've gone through can be overcome, healed, and result in you being a stronger and caring person. I know, because I'm still here.

Before you continue reading, I'd like to ask you a favor. If you are depressed or live with someone battling depression or suicidal thoughts and you have a gun in the house, please get rid of it. It doesn't have to be forever. But please, please, please, make it difficult for yourself or someone you love to do something stupid.

The world needs Dr. Lulu and people like her. People willing to talk about things most people would rather avoid. *The best way to prevent suicide is to talk about it.*

The world needs more people like you, too. People willing to have the hard conversations and read books that can save lives.

Be well, and enjoy life,

Andy Grant

Author, Coach, and Suicide Attempt Survivor

TheAndyGrant.com

Part 1

Facts, Figures, The Foundation

In 2015, WHO announced that the ***stigma*** of mental illness is
"a global public health crisis."

Chapter 1

MY WHY

I shall begin with a trip back to the year 2000, when I had my very first personal encounter with suicide. She was a friend, a colleague, a surgery resident and a fellow Nigerian. She was 33 years old. I hadn't checked up on her in a while, she had been on my mind, but I kept putting it off. I kept finding one excuse or the other not to check in with her. I was 7 months pregnant and had been dealing with some complications with the pregnancy. Finally, that Sunday morning I picked up the phone and dialed her number. The voice on the other end sounded surprised and a little hesitant. When I explained that I was her long-time friend and colleague, out of nowhere (as if trying to get it over and done with) she blurted out *"my aunty blew her brains out 2 weeks ago!"* The shock from the news put me into preterm labor, and my now 19-year-old son was born 6 weeks early. I eventually got over the incident, and carried on with my life, business as usual. I assumed it was a one-time thing, that it was never going to happen again. Not to me. Not to any of my friends or anyone I know, and definitely not to any of my patients. I was wrong.

In 2008, I experienced my first patient suicide. He had been severely depressed, a quarterback in his high school football team. The only son of his parents. He was only 15 years old. He had come to see me in March of that year in the company of his mother. She was concerned that he had lost interest in football, a game he was not only very good at, but also really loved. She wanted me to *"check him for drugs."* After checking him out, and spending some time interviewing him and administering the proper screening, I told his mom my findings. He had severe depression, and I recommended medications and therapy. She turned them both down, stating that he was going to be *"just fine,"* because she had a family history of depression and they had all *"done okay."* On July 4th that year (only three months after I first made the diagnosis), during the family barbecue, he walked out into the front lawn, placed a double-barrel shotgun in his mouth and pulled the trigger. I will never forget the look in his mother's eyes when she came back to the office to tell me the story... The color and lights were gone... Forever.

In 2018, I had a visit from a 7yr old patient of mine who has ADHD. His mom brought him to see me because he had attempted to hang himself in their home, twice. In his defense, he had uncontrolled ADHD and a strong family history of mental illness.

4

He was on medication, but he wasn't compliant. Though he didn't die, a part of me died that day. The part that goes to the office every day to see patients and write prescriptions for coughs and colds. The part that would perform physicals, give advice on asthma or treat strep throat. The part that was a *"regular doctor."* That encounter has changed the course of my life forever.

I must also add that in the 10 years between the suicided patient and the 7year old, I noticed an increase in the number of patients (children, teens and young adults) presenting to my office with anxiety, cutting, depression, suicidal thoughts and attempts. The combination of my patients and the almost daily news of child and youth suicides led me to the decision to quit clinical medicine in 2018. I started blogging, speaking and writing to create awareness and educate the world on youth suicide and haven't looked back. In addition, I started a podcast, Suicide Pages with Dr. Lulu earlier this year (found on all platforms you listen to your favorite podcasts) to further help me with my mission. By reading this book, you are also assisting with the mission, and for that, I am grateful ☺.

Chapter 2

SUICIDE DEFINED

According to the National Institute of Mental Health (NIMH), *suicide* is defined as death caused by a purposeful self-directed injurious behavior, *with an intent to die* as a result of the behavior. Next only to accidents, suicide is the second leading cause of death for youth in most countries, civilized or uncivilized. Mind you, it is possible that some suicides have been ruled as accidents, because most times we don't truly know the motives behind them.

One could argue that in very young children such as my 7-year-old patient, there is a limit to the understanding of the finality of self-directed injurious behavior, or the fact that their actions will really lead to death. Though research studies have shown that children as young as 4-6 years do understand the finality of death, my argument is that they might not completely comprehend that a certain act *will* cause them to die. For instance, they might get that their dead pet goldfish is never coming home, or that their previously ailing grandparent is *"in heaven,"* but they might not understand that the belt or jump rope tied tightly around their neck might cause them to never come back.

Take for example, the kids who died playing the choking game, also called *"Flatliner," "Space Monkey"* or *"Pass-out-challenge."* Over 1,400 deaths were recorded as having resulted from that game between 2000 and 2015, before the Centers for Disease Control (CDC), stopped collating them. Kids play the game for the thrill, to get high. However, it *is* asphyxiation, and it *is* very dangerous. Blood supply to the brain is *always* cut off during the game. It often only takes seconds to minutes before brain damage sets in, so they are in essence, playing with the proverbial fire each time they engage in the act. One such kid, 14-year-old Carson Steele of Rock Hill, South Carolina who died, had recorded himself playing the game several times. The last time he played it, he actually declared on camera *"I hope I don't get hurt."* That declaration is my point exactly, he did not believe he would get hurt, he did not believe he could *die* from it… Sadly, a quick YouTube search turns up more than 36 million results for *"how to play pass out game"* and more than half a million more for *"how to play choking game,"* which include everything from news reports to homemade tutorials.

So, who is to say that many of the deaths by say, motor vehicles, or drowning or even overdoses were accidental? One of the symptoms of suicidal behavior is recklessness, in teens this could manifest as engaging in high risk behaviors. While we might

7

rule them as *"normal teen behavior,"* who is to say they are not suicidal attempts? More than one of the guests on my podcast confided that they had engaged in many high-risk activities in an attempt to end their lives, luckily, they didn't die, but what if they had? Would we have ruled their deaths as accidents or as suicides? I think you get my point ☺. So, my definition of suicide includes both *"purposeful intent to die* as well as *accidental death from the actions."* This point further argues that the current quoted numbers of suicides per year are most likely far less than the actual numbers.

Definitions / Words Do Matter

Suicidal ideation refers to thinking about, considering, or planning suicide.

Suicidal behavior is an act or a group or activities that can lead to suicide. It can include preparation (giving away stuff, saying goodbye), collecting means (buying a gun, getting pills together) or simply writing a suicide note.

Suicide attempt is a non-fatal, self-directed, potentially injurious behavior with an intent to die as a result of the behavior, but such behavior might not always result in injury or death.

Suicide contagion refers to the process by which the exposure to suicide or suicidal behaviors within one's family, one's peer group, or through media reports of suicide can result in an increase in suicidal behaviors and suicide in persons *at risk*. Reports have shown that adolescents are often the most at risk. A suicide contagion can lead to a suicide cluster.

Suicide cluster is defined as a group of suicides, suicide attempts or both, that occur closer together in time and geographical location than would normally be expected based on statistical prediction or community expectation.

Chapter 3

SUICIDE 101

Did you know that according to the World Health Organization (WHO) statistics, more than 800,000 people globally die by suicide each year? That translates roughly to one suicide every 40 seconds! Suicide claims more lives than malaria, breast cancer, war and homicide. However, since many suicides still go unreported mostly due to stigma, it is highly likely that-that number is underestimated. For instance, suicides in minorities, developing countries, most conservative communities, Indigenous and rural or remote parts of the world are not reported. Imagine if we could obtain accurate numbers, and somehow count every suicide in the whole world, how many would there then be? One every second? The WHO has called it a *"serious global public health issue,"* and yet, only 38 countries in the world have suicide prevention strategies laid out. Believe it or not, in 2018, the WHO predicted that by the year 2020, at the current rate, there will be one suicide every 20 seconds! Imagine that! A world where one precious life is lost to suicide every 20 seconds! What kind of world would that be? And that is not considering all the accidental, or unreported suicides, because I strongly believe that many accidental deaths were suicides.

So, what if there were a pandemic of a deadly virus outbreak that kills one person every 20 to 40 seconds, what do you think people would do? My guess is everyone would be up in arms, running for cover, looking for an antidote, right? Unfortunately, SUICIDE *is* that deadly virus today, yet, much of the world looks the other way, pretends not to care, completely ignores it or is largely silent about it. Making the stigma even worse.

Suicide characteristics differ based on a country's economic status. Overall, more men die by suicide than women, then again there are variations based on the economic status of the country. In richer countries, three times more men die by suicide than women, but in low- and middle-income countries this ratio is 1.5 men to each woman. In most western countries, suicide rates are highest in middle-aged men and men 70 years and over, but young people aged 15-29 are also particularly vulnerable.

Did you know that the National Alliance on Mental Illness (NAMI) states 1 in 5 adults in the US (46.6 million) experiences mental illness each year? Yep, that's the going statistic. Apparently 1 in 25 adults in the United States (US) experiences a serious mental illness that substantially interferes with or limits one or more major life activities each year. As one can imagine, these numbers are substantially higher when we include the youth and the younger generation. Please note that ***mental illness is only one of the risk factors for suicide.*** Suicide is a very complex thing and factors like genetics, untreated mental illness, substance abuse, racism, bullying, inequality, lack of access to mental healthcare, easy access to guns etc. all play significant roles in it.

Ultimately, *despair, and not depression* (as Big Pharma would have you think), is the root cause for suicide. I can explain. In recent years, the diagnoses of depression have increased, and antidepressant prescriptions in the US have more than paralleled that increase. If these medications are indeed effective, why then are suicide rates increasing? Why is depression blamed every time a suicide death occurs? The truth is life's challenges when piled up against a person (already at risk), can often lead them to despair, hopelessness and suicidal ideation, and if that person happens upon a means to carry out the act, suicide occurs. No type, or dose of an antidepressant can fix that root cause. While they might present with reactive or secondary depression from their problems, treating just the depression without treating its cause or providing coping skills will only worsen the situation. Especially since a common side effect of antidepressants *is* suicidal ideation. Many child and teen suicides we hear about in the news stem from bullying, can antidepressants do anything about that?

Have you ever heard about Adverse Childhood Experiences (ACEs)? Do you know what your ACEs score is? Do you know if you have a risk for suicide attempts? Did you know that certain significantly traumatic events that occurred in your childhood can increase your risk of certain illnesses and suicide? ACEs are severely traumatic childhood events that harm children's developing brains. They lead to a change in how children respond to stress and damage their immune systems so profoundly that the effects show up in late teen and adult years.

ACEs have been found to be at the core of many adult illnesses. In children, recent studies have shown that ACEs, especially when cumulative, can increase teen and adult suicide risk by up to 1220%! Even one single ACE score can increase the risk of suicide attempt by 5 times. I had never heard about ACEs until Dr. Nadine Burke's TED talk. Today, she is on a mission to reduce the ACEs scores of all children, in order to help ameliorate all the health consequences that can occur as a result. You can find a copy of an ACEs questionnaire in the appendix of this book. Please take the test and document your score. It might illuminate some things for you. If not, it will at least help you get a better understanding of your life and your health challenges.

The landmark study on ACEs was done by Kaiser Permanente in conjunction with the CDC between 1995 and 1997. It was a longitudinal study of adults to evaluate the effects of significant trauma in their childhood and subsequent occurrence of certain diseases in adulthood. The events must have occurred before the age of 18 to count. What they found was an overwhelming correlation between the following childhood traumatic events: *physical, sexual, and emotional abuse. Family history of mental illness, incarceration, domestic abuse, physical and emotional neglect. Family history of divorce or suicidality,* **and** *the incidence and prevalence of heart disease, obesity,* *chronic lung disease, cancer, substance abuse, autoimmune diseases, behavior problems, learning disabilities and suicide.* For me, this finding hit close to home, because my own children have at least two risk factors, parental divorce and domestic abuse. And I personally was sexually assaulted when I was only 9 years old.

Other factors that increase the risk of suicidality, especially in children and youth, include:

- A history of bullying
- Relationship issues like breakups
- Previous suicide attempt*
- LGBTQ+ sexual orientation
- Access to lethal weapons in the home
- Behavior problems like ADHD/ADD
- Poverty
- Socioeconomic/sociocultural oppression
- Institutional racism
- Lack of access to treatment and support for mental illness
- Substance Abuse
- Microaggressions like police brutality and racial profiling
- Social Media
- Lack of Support at home and at school
- Suicide in peers and in the community (suicide contagion)

* A prior suicide attempt is the single most important risk factor for a future death by suicide.

Chapter 4

AROUND THE WORLD IN SUICIDE

In 2015, the National Crime Records Bureau (NCRB) declared that *"**every hour one student commits suicide in India**"*. Was that a quizzical look on your face? Yep, that was the exact reaction I had when I first read it too. Suicide is apparently the leading cause of death in Indian Youth aged 15-39 years. Did you know that 37% of women who die by suicide in the world are Indian? Or that Indian men account for 24% of cases of suicide worldwide? These words were the title of an article published in the Times of India in September of 2018. Did you know this? I had no idea! India has one of the highest suicide rates in the entire world. Alas, I wish that were all. Regrettably, India is not alone in this. I bet you also didn't know that the US and many other countries also record very high suicide numbers.

In January 2019, Australian newspapers reported a total of 5 suicides in Indigenous teens aged 12-15 years in the space of 9 days. Other news sources reported 35 deaths in the space of 3 months also in their Indigenous population, including three 12 year olds. In Australia, the overall suicide rate in 2015 was 12.6 per 100,000, that was the highest rate in 10-plus years, about 8 deaths by suicide per day. Like that isn't bad enough, suicide in the United States has surged to the highest levels in nearly 30 years, with increases in every age group. Approximately 1 in 25 teenagers in the United States has attempted suicide, and as many as 1 in 8 has contemplated suicide. In May of 2018, the New York Times reported that African American children aged 5 to 11 years are twice as likely as their Caucasian counterparts to die by suicide. And in October of 2019, an updated study upheld these findings. *One child in this age group dies of suicide every 5 days.* While the youngest child ever reported to have died by suicide was a five 5-year-old Chinese girl, in the US, there were two 6 year old girls, one Black and one White. Fueled by the **3S's (silence, stigma and shame)** suicide is now the second leading cause of death for children aged 10 to 34 years in the US.

Did you know that Latino teens in the US have very high rates of suicide attempts? Another huge surprise for me. The peak age for suicide attempts for this ethnic group is 14 to 15 years. According to the CDC, nearly 26% of Latino adolescents have considered suicide. 15% of them have attempted suicide one or more times, compared to 9.8% of their Caucasian, and10.2% of their Black counterparts respectively. This statistic became clearer to me when in October 2018, I attended my first Out of the

Darkness walk in San Antonio, Texas. 98% of the nearly 300 families that registered and walked that day, were Hispanic.

Believe it or not, in some cultures (Asian, Islamic and even Western cultures), suicide is an acceptable and rational response to shame. In cultures like this, the suicide rates are not only high, Suicide is actually encouraged as a way out of personal failures or what might seem to be life's unsolvable difficulties. *"Seppuku,"* a form of suicide in Ancient Japanese Samurai culture was long considered an honorable act of self-resolve such that despite the removal of cultural sanctioning, the rate of suicide in Japan remains high with suicide masquerading as seppuku still being carried out by its citizens both there and abroad. Despite persistent counter-opinions, euthanasia and physician-assisted suicide in the context of terminal illness is increasingly accepted as a way to preserve autonomy and dignity in the West. Suicide as an act of murder and terrorism is a practice currently popular with Islamic militants who regard it as martyrdom in the context of war.

According to the CDC reports, Alaskan Native and American Indian (AN/AI) youth aged 15 to 24 years have the highest rate of suicidal behavior of all the US races! Let's take a quick look at the statistics. Unlike the general US population in which suicide rates increase with age, suicide rates decline with age for AI/AN indigenes. The Indian Health Services (IHS) Trends in Indian Health report (2014), which provides data on AI/AN indigenes who reside in IHS service areas, identified suicide as the second leading cause of death for their youth of that age group. The data reports that the male suicide rate was more than 31/2 times the suicide rate for males of all races in that age group. While rates for females in that age group though lower than males, was still nearly six times the rate for females of all races. More than one-third of Native American suicide deaths were youth.

In the great continent of Africa where I am from, suicide is slowly making headlines nearly daily. While Lesotho has the highest suicide rate in Africa, in the past few years and months, Nigerian and Kenyan youth have also taken the forefront in this. In Kenya, university students are dying at an alarming rate, and a great majority of the victims are men. According to the WHO, the number of suicides reported in Kenya rose by 58% between 2008 and 2017, a ten-year high. Suicide rates in university students in Nigeria mirror those in Kenya. Unfortunately, suicide and mental health issues like depression, are still a huge taboo and even a crime in most African countries. Risk factors are similar for suicide and suicide attempts in these countries, they include failed relationships, mental and physical health problems, family conflicts, socioeconomic problems and drug and alcohol use/abuse. Globally, 55% of suicide victims are aged 15 to 44 years.

Chapter 5

SUICIDE AND CHILDREN/YOUTH (OF INDIGENOUS POPULATIONS)

(Adapted from studies on Indigenous Australian Youth)

There is something especially shocking about the suicide of a child, because for them, life is just beginning. It indicates serious underlying issues in our society, and our children are reacting to their environments. Children may be at higher risk of suicide if they experience ACEs that contribute to major psychological distress, before the age of 18yr, as discussed earlier. In the short term, we must identify and provide immediate help to our children and young people in crisis situations. Families, peers and schools must be involved, with backup from counsellors and, if required, 24/7 access to culturally competent mental health professionals. The plan must also address child sexual abuse that is increasingly associated with suicide.

Any sustainable response must go to the deeper, underlying historical causes of hopelessness and despair which contribute to suicide. This isn't just a problem among children, it is often a communal problem. Furthermore, it is not a mental health issue. A diagnosed mental illness is present in only about half of those who die by suicide. Deeper causes include intergenerational trauma in the form of poverty, racism, social exclusion, substandard housing, and economic marginalization of communities. These are the legacies of colonization and drive the suicide rates in the Indigenous populace.

Indigenous youth suicide is different because it cannot be separated from the historical and related present-day situations. Other Indigenous people from around the world share similar histories and high rates of child and youth suicide. This has become obvious as studies look at suicide rates in African American, Native American and Indigenous Australian and Canadian children. We know, for instance, that factors such as substance abuse and unemployment elevate the risk of suicide for Indigenous and non-Indigenous people. It is however widely acknowledged that these risk factors are more prevalent in the Indigenous population than the non-Indigenous population. There is no question that better efforts are needed to address avoidable risk factors for suicide. As a social issue, suicide is entwined with tangible and intangible influences of gender, ethnicity, connectedness, and mental and physical well-being. Above and beyond this already complex network of influences, Indigenous suicide is linked with difficult questions of colonization, dispossession, racism and social marginalization.

Many of the issues faced in Indigenous communities, which elevate the risk of suicide, have their roots deep in inter-generational suffering. But there are also unique aspects of Indigenous society and culture that offer hope for the future in reducing the burden of suicide mortality. Indigenous societies like the Native American and other minority societies, promote social cohesion, extended familial ties and spontaneous support, which can all lower the risk of suicide. By re-integrating group identity, feelings of empowerment, repossession and community pride into the lives of Indigenous people, these protective characteristics can be given the chance to re-emerge and flourish.

Chapter 6

SUICIDE FYI

As one might imagine, suicide has a devastating impact on families, friends and entire communities. However, ***it can largely be prevented***. Modern social scientist Emile Durkheim described suicide as one of the *"crudest expressions of social phenomenon."* One blogger who attempted suicide and survived, describes it as a state of *"ultimate human burnout."* He believes people who attempt suicide are emotionally exhausted and feel like they have used up all their options to live, and at that moment, they also have a means to carry it out.

The decision to end one's life is not an easy one, it is generally not something that happens at the spur of the moment or based on just one situation. Many times, it is a culmination of overwhelming life's stressors and a lack of options to solve them. Many times, these people are trapped by events in their lives. One blogger compared it to his entire body being on fire and he needing to put it out.

After many suicides, a psychological autopsy is often performed. It is a valuable tool in research. It involves collecting all available information on the deceased via structural interviews of family members, relatives or friends as well as their healthcare providers, psychiatric records, forensic examinations and school authorities etc. It essentially helps better estimate the role of the various risk factors for suicide in the deceased, like undiagnosed or undertreated mental health disorders, substance abuse or other emotional issues.

So, I ask for compassion from you as you read the stories of the teens in this book. I ask that you try to understand them from their points of view, remembering that what breaks me, might not necessarily break you. Their lives and their decisions are not for you to judge, but to try to comprehend. Ultimately, I ask that you stay open minded and be empathetic. *Try* to see their worlds from a different viewpoint than yours: one of less judgement and more mindfulness, less impatience and more kindness, less prejudice and more love.

Chapter 7

MORE SUICIDE STATS.

- More teenagers and young adults die from suicide than from cancer, heart disease, AIDS, birth defects, stroke, pneumonia, influenza, and chronic lung disease *combined.*
- Each day in the US, there are an average of over 3,000 suicide attempts by young people in grades 9-12.
- About 100 teens and young adults die each week from suicide in the US.
- According to the CDC's 2017 Youth Risk Behavioral Survey one in fourteen young people in the US attempted suicide in the previous 12 months. The good news is that thirteen out of fourteen did not attempt. But one is too many. What if that one happens to be your child, grandchild, your best friend, or the young person next door?

- *Four out of five teens who attempt suicide give clear warning signs.* This point is so important because most of us either don't know / recognize the warning signs or ignore them when we see them. They include other suicide attempts, giving away their belongings, asking questions about death or suicide, writing a suicide note, buying a gun etc. There are a few cases of suicided teens who appeared to have left no signs though. One such teen that comes to mind is Ms. Alexandra Valoras. However, a closer look at Ms. Valoras' story shows a teenaged girl who appeared to be thriving, but after her death, her parents discovered her 200-page journal full of self-hatred, self-loathing and suicidal thoughts.

Chapter 8

GUNS AND SUICIDE

If you live in the US, then you know first-hand the devastation that can be caused by a gun. Our TV screens are inundated with mass shooting, after mass shooting, after mass shooting. Did you know that the US leads the world in child gun deaths? It makes sense though, right? In the US we have the National Rifle Association (NRA) which is behind most gun ownership laws. Here, even well-meaning gun owners can be affected by the death of a loved one from keeping guns in the home. There are studies, statistics and facts that stress the inherent danger associated with leaving such deadly weapons within reach. Believe it or not, 4.6 million children in the US live in homes with unlocked or loaded guns. And three in four of these children know where the guns are stored in their home. Luckily, the American Academy of Pediatrics (AAP) and other organizations like Moms Demand Action are in the fight and advocating for more commonsense gun laws.

According to the Ad Council, 8 children die from accidental gun deaths in the US every day. Among children, the majority (89%) of unintentional shooting deaths happen in the home. Most of them occur when children are playing with a loaded gun in their parents' absence. People who own or report firearm access have twice the risk of homicide and more than three times the risk of suicide compared to those who don't. Suicide rates are much higher in states with higher rates of gun ownership, even after controlling for differences in poverty, urbanization, unemployment, mental illness, and substance abuse. Statistics have shown that the presence of a handgun in a home often results in a serious or fatal injury to a family member in the home. The term *"Family Fire"* was developed by the campaign for gun safety. It refers to a shooting involving an improperly stored or misused gun found in the home that results in the death or injury of a loved one or family member. Incidents include unintentional shootings, suicides and other gun-related tragedies. I state these numbers because not only are 58% of suicides by firearms, firearms are also the most common method of suicide by most American youth except the AI/AN youth who mostly die by suffocation from hanging. The importance of gun safety cannot be overemphasized.

Chapter 9

SOME COMMON TEEN ISSUES

As if adolescence is not confusing and stressful enough, teens also deal with a myriad of other issues. Some of the commoner ones like self-harm, eating disorders, identity crises etc. are discussed below. We are mainly looking at those that relate to the stories of the teens we shall be learning about later. This list is not in the least bit exhaustive, but it is an introduction to their deeper, often more complex struggles that will hopefully foster a healthy discussion in the home or at school.

<u>Self-Harm</u>

In 2008, researchers at Yale University reported that 56% of 10 to 14-year-old girls they interviewed admitted to having engaged in Non-Suicidal Self Injury (NSSI) at some point in their lifetime. This number rose by 36% in 2018. There is no current consensus as to whether these girls are depressed, suicidal, or attention-seeking. What we know for now is NSSI is a way of coping with painful emotions, and bad situations. Sufferers claim they get relief from their bad feelings when they engage in the behavior. Some report that it helps them numb the emotional pain they are going through, while others report that it simply helps them feel something, anything. Some see it as a form of self-punishment, while some believe that the endorphins released during the tissue injury brings a calming effect and emotional relief. As you can see, the etiology is complex and still needs more research.

People self-injure regardless of race and socioeconomic status. According to a New York Times article from July of 2018, about 1 in 4 white adolescent females compared to 1 in 10 white adolescent males engage in self-harming behavior, and the numbers are as high as 30% of females in certain parts of the country. In the US, the overall prevalence of self-harming behavior is about 18% nationwide. Depending on the study, rates have been quoted to be highest in Asian Americans, some say the prevalence is highest in Native American students, while one CDC study reported that 12% of Black students engage in self-injury. Clearly, a lot more research is needed in this field.

Homosexuality

Did you know that the average Nigerian household believes a gay or homosexual child is a curse to the family? They believe that the child is somehow defective, a disgrace to the family and some even consider them outcasts. A recent survey shows that 90% of Nigerians support the Same Sex Marriage Prohibition Act

(SSMPA). An Act that was signed into existence in 2014 (by then president Goodluck Jonathan) heralding widespread attacks, arrests and jailing of many LGBTQ+ individuals or their sympathizers. The Islamic religion with its Sharia law system also prohibits any same sex unions, with perpetrators facing the wrath of up to a 10 to14-year jail term, or public flogging with oil-soaked hide whips as a deterrent of their orientation. Christians preach strongly against the lifestyle claiming it is from the devil. These people are often called misfits, witches, predators, and the scum of the earth to name a few. Consequently, young Nigerians who find themselves members of the community have pretty much nowhere to go. Some are completely disowned by their family members, while some run away from home and become wards of the society facing homelessness and the menace of the streets.

Substance use and abuse is easy to embrace for these youth as a result of this persecution and discrimination. When we add poor healthcare access to the mix, they become high risk for diseases like HIV infection. Globally, sex trafficking, kidnapping, or murder are also commonplace, and suicide is slowly becoming an avenue of escape for LGBTQ+ youth all over the world. In Nigeria/Africa, those who unfortunately contract the HIV virus face a life of certain death with little or no availability of drug treatment.

Even in so-called civilized countries, stigma, rejection and ostracization of members of the LGBTQ+ community are very rampant. In other words, it is not an issue found only in developing countries. For instance, in recent news, the US has been leading the pack in homicides involving the transgender community. Unfortunately, a great majority of these victims are African American. In 2017, anti LGBTQ+ homicides nearly doubled according to the National Coalition of Anti-Violence Programs (NCAVP). Here are some names of some victims of hate killings in the US for 2018 and 2019 respectively, adapted from the Human Rights Campaign (HRC). Recently, Twitter was abuzz with the news of a trans woman who was burned to death in her car in South Florida, this kind of deadly outcome is fueled by hate. As a result of this type of hate, stigma, and ostracization, many members of this community remain in the closet, and they very often don't access care even from the medical community and these factors easily lead to depression, feelings of alienation, hopelessness, despair and ultimately increases their suicide rates.

Eating Disorders

Eating disorders include: Anorexia Nervosa (AN), Bulimia Nervosa and Binge Eating Disorder. They are relatively common and serious complex conditions that affect teens and young adults. While they largely occur more in females, males are also often affected. In the US where there is a preponderance of obsession with weight, eating disorders are reported to affect millions of teens. Researches document roughly 1in 7 females are struggling with an eating disorder at any point in time. Over one third (36%) of adolescent females surveyed believe they are overweight, and 59% are actively, or have actively tried to lose weight.

According to WebMD, eating disorders have multiple etiological factors. They range from: genetics, early childhood trauma, peer pressure, dysfunctional family dynamics, to criticism. Social media and other forms of media that glorify weight loss or skinny body habitus also play a huge role. Teens that participate in sporting activities where weight is monitored, those who have very high personal expectations or are obsessed with perfection are also at risk for developing eating disorders.

Symptoms include, vomiting after meals, excessive preoccupation with weight, refusing to eat, excessive use of laxatives or diuretics, eating low-calorie foods, binge eating, excessive exercise, and an altered body image, whereby the person sees themselves as always overweight irrespective of their current weight. Parents should look out for teeth marks on their teen's knuckle areas caused manually induced vomiting. In advanced stages, sufferers may present with irregular menstrual cycles, mood swings, hair loss, and irregular heart rhythms which can cause death.

By estimation, >10 million people in the US suffer from eating disorders, and though it is fast becoming more prevalent in other western countries, many sufferers of these disorders keep them a secret or are often in denial, so our current statistics might be misleading. In countries like Japan, AN cases are now 10 times higher than they were 30 years ago. Bulimia which apparently had no reported cases 40 years ago, is now the country's biggest eating disorder problem.

Drug or Alcohol Abuse

Experimentation with drugs is a surefire way to addiction for many-a-teen. This behavior is very common in early to mid-teen years when peer pressure is often a strong presence in their lives. Teens generally don't like to be different, they want to conform to their peers, sometimes without considering all the consequences. Even with adequate parental guidance, teenagers still often experience fear of missing out (FOMO) where their friends and peers are concerned, and often cave into peer pressure. They want to dress alike, talk alike, and act alike, even if it involves high-risk behaviors. Very often, disappointments, poor school performance, social pressures, and suboptimal family dynamics can push them to experiment with drugs like tobacco, alcohol, vaping, etc. if offered by their friends. These seemingly innocent habits could rapidly lead to addiction.

With the advent of vaping (e-cigarettes), (the prototype is called the *Juul*. It looks like a flash drive and can be charged in a laptop computer), teens are now using this as a substitute for regular smoking, and more and more of them are becoming addicted to it. They come in attractive cases, and all kinds of interesting flavors. Some promise no nicotine, while others promise only water and flavors like Cinnamon. However, like anything else being marketed to adolescents, they are now being laced with CBD oils, Marijuana, and even Opioids. Recent news reports have linked vaping to mysterious lung infections and illnesses that have puzzled doctors and caregivers. There has also been overdosing by teens who smoked unknown substances laced with noxious chemicals. And tragically, there have been reports of death as a result of vaping.

Teen Pregnancy

According to the CDC, since the early 1990s, teen birth rates have continued to decline in the United States. It hit an all-time low in 2017. These numbers (though good news and saving the public up to $4.4 billion in 2015) are still substantially higher than in other western industrialized nations. There is also a huge ethnic and racial disparity in the statistics. Depending on the literature examined, Hispanic teens or Alaskan/Indian teens might have the highest rate of pregnancy. Per the CDC, the decreasing numbers are as a result of increased abstinence behavior and use of birth control resulting from intense grassroots efforts. However, much work is still to be done to close the racial and ethnic disparities.

Poor education, low-income levels, less opportunities for positive youth development, neighborhood racial segregation and income inequality are all determinants of the racial disparities. To eliminate them, we need to increase funding for, and synergize with community programs in the low income and Indigenous underserved areas, in order to provide or improve their current preventive healthcare practices. We must improve health education, improve youth access to existing services, continue partnering with community and government programs, and overall, continue educating our teens and the community at large to further the process along (see part 2 of this book for further discussion.)

Family Dynamics and Relationship Issues

Misunderstandings with parents and close family members, and relationship issues with their peers are the most important risk factors for emotional wellness in adolescents. For instance, Latino teens reportedly butt heads frequently with their parents as a result of differences in opinions and mindsets. Generational misunderstandings uniquely present themselves in many of these families as a result of immigration. These first-generation teens often find themselves feeling isolated, confused and depressed because their immigrant parents have a more traditional mindset. They have a more Americanized mindset leading to clashes in expectations and outcomes. Many of these teens are believed by experts to engage in self-harm as a result of the family discord, partially explaining the high rates of suicide attempts and suicides.

As an immigrant parent and mother of three first generation Nigerian-Americans, I have experienced this difference in generational mindsets first-hand. There are certain things my children do and get away with, that I would never have thought about doing as a child growing up in Nigeria. One such thing is looking me straight in the eye and talking back or arguing. While my children don't see it as anything weird, I on the other hand, would *never* have been able to look any grown adult, (certainly not my parents), in the eye, let alone argue with them! I grew up in a very traditional Nigerian home, and nothing like that would ever have happened. Yet, my children do it, and it's not a big deal to them. While it doesn't necessarily have major negative outcomes, it is certainly a generational difference between us.

Teen Dating, Teen Domestic Violence and Suicide

Okay, either I am in the group of most naïve adults out there, or I am living under a nice comfortable rock, because I had no idea there were teen dating sites, or did I? Lol. Either way, I only found this out while writing this book. The good news is that in the past few years, high school teens report a decrease in dating overall, with record lows in 2017. According to childtrends.org, although dating in adolescence is still common, students in the eighth, tenth, and twelfth grades in 2017 were less likely to report dating than their counterparts were in 1992.

Relationship violence is, however, a common problem faced by adolescents in the United States and in many other countries across the globe. It can occur in same sex as well as heterosexual relationships. In general, adolescents are at higher risk for relationship victimization than adults, and females between the ages of 16 and 24 years are at the highest risk of relationship victimization. Teenage dating violence is just as serious as adult domestic violence, especially because it often starts a pattern of abuse or victimization that can last a lifetime. Also, the severity of intimate partner violence in adulthood is often greater in cases where the pattern of abuse was established in adolescence.

Victimized adolescents are at higher risk for planning and/or attempting suicide compared to non-victimized adolescents.

Dating violence can take place in person or electronically, such as repeated texting or posting sexual pictures of a partner online without consent. Unhealthy relationships can start early and can persist if no help is offered in a timely fashion.

Teens often think some behaviors, like teasing and name-calling, are a *"normal"* part of a relationship—but these behaviors can become abusive and develop into serious forms of violence. However, many teens don't report unhealthy behaviors because they are afraid to tell family and friends for fear of backlash. So, we as parents must have a high index of suspicion.

Male students who experience both physical and sexual teen dating violence were about twice as likely to have attempted suicide in the previous 12 months than are females.

- **Physical violence** is when a person hurts or tries to hurt a partner by hitting, kicking, or using another type of physical force.
- **Sexual violence** is forcing or attempting to force a partner to take part in a sex act, sexual touching, or a non-physical sexual event (e.g., sexting) when the partner does not or cannot consent.
- **Psychological aggression** is the use of verbal and non-verbal communication with the intent to harm another person mentally or emotionally and/or exert control over another person.

- **Stalking** is a pattern of repeated, unwanted attention and contact by a partner that causes fear or concern for one's own safety or the safety of someone close to the victim.

Consequences of Teen Dating Violence

- Symptoms of depression and anxiety
- Engaging in unhealthy behaviors, like using tobacco, drugs, and alcohol
- Exhibiting antisocial behaviors, like lying, theft, bullying or hitting
- Thinking about suicide or even attempting suicide

Teens who are controlling are also likely to start reading their partner's texts and going through their phone, they may also send threats over text. Teenagers are also more likely to engage in sexting—sending inappropriate pictures and messages. This isn't necessarily unhealthy but can become a means of abuse—either the abuser sending and forcing their partner to look at images or coercing the victim into sending photos or messages that could be shared or used as a threat.

Quick Note: Did you know that sexting, though not a crime per se, can have legal consequences? Any exchange of nude photos or videos of someone under 18 could be considered child pornography, which is always illegal. Even if whoever sent the image did so willingly, the recipient can still get in a lot of trouble.

So, please stress the need to avoid nude picture at all costs, to your teens.

Chapter 10

AMERICAN FOUNDATION FOR SUICIDE PREVENTION (AFSP)

Have you ever heard about *#talksaveslives* or *#silencekills?* They are the two hashtags utilized by the American Foundation for Suicide Prevention (AFSP) in their campaigns for suicide prevention and suicide awareness. AFSP is an all-volunteer organization with a mission to give those affected by suicide a nationwide community empowered by research, education and advocacy to act against this leading cause of death. It is dedicated to saving lives and bringing hope to those affected by suicide.

The biggest problems most communities face are the **silence, shame and stigma** or taboo surrounding mental illness (especially depression) and suicide. These three factors are the greatest threats to effective mental healthcare delivery in today's world. Most adults who suffer from mental ill-health are often ashamed to go to the doctor. They are afraid of owning the diagnosis. They worry about what people will say, how they will be perceived. They fear backlash from work, ostracization from their friends, and invariably end up untreated, or inadequately treated. Even doctors who have the highest rates of suicides suffer a similar fate. They fear professional backlash from their peers and the medical boards. This situation is considerably worse when it comes to teens and young adults. They also fear teasing or bullying from their friends and family members, and so no one wants to talk about it. Yet we know research has shown that talking about our problems is lifesaving, and silence causes worsening of the situation, hence the hashtags. The responsibility therefore rests primarily on us as the *"village / tribe"* of our loved ones to be mindful and supportive. We must be aware of our words, our actions and our body language around our teens if they do confide in us about their mental ill-health or suicidality.

Alternatively, we could broach the topic, approach them and ask the difficult questions like *"Do you feel like the world would be better off without you?" "Have you ever thought about ending your life?" "Would you ever consider hurting yourself?"* When we do ask the questions, we must be willing to receive their responses and act appropriately without judgement.

~We must offer a listening ear and a helping hand and stay with them to help them feel safe.

~Get rid of any potential weapons of harm and offer to take them to see the appropriate healthcare provider.

~Offer appropriate suggestions to help with coping and dealing with the situations that cause their present state of mind if we can.

~Most importantly, no judgement.

Imagine a world where the shame and stigma attached to depression and suicide are permanently erased. A world where talking about one's depression could someday become the norm, an okay thing, an in-thing, maybe even a movement. Perhaps following in the footsteps of hashtags like *#metoo* for sexual assault victims, or *#nomoresilence* for victims of domestic abuse. A world where we could make the *#talksaveslives* or *#silencekills* movements bigger.

Do you know that many people who suffer from chronic diseases ultimately end up with depression? Yes, look it up. Many patients with chronic illnesses end up manifesting with depressive symptoms. What I am saying is, if depression is ultimately unavoidable with chronic illness, then the sooner we embrace it, the better.

Imagine a world where depression is viewed as an ordinary *"health condition"* rather than a *"mental health condition."* Simply referring to it as a chronic illness, like asthma, diabetes or lupus, rather than mental illness will go a long way in removing the stigma, eliminating the shame, and abolishing the silence. I say, why not? Why should one person's asthma be more important than the other person's depression? Or my arthritis be more openly acceptable than your schizophrenia? As a parent, why should it be ok for you to talk openly about your son's head injury than I about my daughter's bipolar disorder?

So, together let us *#EndtheSilenceShameandStigmaofSuicide*.

Chapter 11

DEPRESSION, ISOLATION AND US HUMANS

Depression, according to the Diagnostic and Statistical Manual of Mental Disorders (DSM–5) is a disease state where the patient experiences extreme sadness and loss of interest in activities that they once enjoyed. It is a relatively common emotional state, about one in five normal people can experience depression in a lifetime. Depression can affect the way one thinks, feels, and acts. It can decrease a person's ability to function at home, at work, at school, or at play. Generally, there is also an association of feelings of worthlessness, loneliness, suicidal thoughts or thoughts of death, changes in appetite, sleep disturbances, irritability, and extreme moodiness. These symptoms must be present for two successive weeks to signify depression.

Depression can affect everyone, including children, but it most often begins in teenagers and young adults. It is very prevalent, affecting up to a fifth of the population, about half of whom are teens aged 12-17. For the most part, depression is a silent disease. It is often a very personal journey of suffering and darkness. It causes us to feel sad, *really sad*, and most people choose not to tell anyone about it. It is often isolating, and sufferers do tend to want to be left alone. But research discourages this isolation and encourages engaging in activities that are mood enhancers like exercise, talking, or hanging out with friends, and if need be, medication. Talking to the right person, helps one not only feel better, but also get a different and often better perspective of things.

It is important to note that there are different types of depression. For this book, we shall be focusing on secondary or reactive depression, which is the type that occurs as a result of a primary or underlying problem. I have found that most youth who become suicidal have a form of reactive depression. In other words, focusing on the depression alone will not help the situation. Helping with the primary or underlying cause of their despair is the key thing. For instance, a child who is being bullied in school, will need us to focus on the bullying and its effects on the child, rather than giving an antidepressant. Same with a child who is being sexually molested or abused at home. *We must seek to understand what happened to the child, first,* before starting on medications. Unfortunately, many doctors and mid-level providers are quick to begin antidepressants, but most of these antidepressants have a side effect of worsening suicidal thoughts and behaviors.

In children, depression might go completely undiagnosed, and in teens it can sometimes mimic normal teen behavior or present as high-risk behavior making it hard to recognize and diagnose. Substance abuse can often exacerbate the symptoms of depression in anyone, particularly adolescents. A family history of depression, abuse, or suicide can be a red flag. Some chronic medical conditions like asthma, seasonal allergies, or migraines can also mimic and exacerbate depressive conditions. The death of a close relative or friend, especially by suicide, can trigger depression and suicidal behavior in those who are already at risk.

As humans, we rely on communication, both verbally, and non-verbally as a way of sharing our experiences with each other. Speaking, verbal communication, is fast becoming a thing of the past. It has been over-taken by our personal computers, handheld devices and cell phones. I once heard of a family who text each other while in the home, as a convenient way of communication, like, who does that? When that ability to verbally communicate our feelings, or that need for physical contact is taken away or is lacking, depression can set in.

In the old days, people used to make eye contact and talk to strangers, they would share a good laugh with a random person and even share a meal. These days however, we are all too busy on our cellphones, most children don't know a life without screen time. Families are becoming estranged from each other, and strangers hardly notice or acknowledge each other. Thanks to social media and video games, most people now have more *virtual friends* than real friends. We crave more *followers*, *likes* and *shares* than eye contact, handshakes or hugs. Emojis and memes have replaced facial expressions and human interactions. These days, everyone's head is bowed down looking at their devices, scrolling, swiping or typing away, it is no wonder the world is losing its interpersonal connections.

As a result of excessive use of personal cell phones and social media, cyber bullying has become a household word. Cyber bullies are getting easy access to our innocent children through these personal devices. I call these types of bullies *"keyboard gangstas."* Children are also being exposed to all kinds of *"negative influences"* coming into our homes through YouTube videos. Even the YouTube stars themselves have not been exempt from the effects of mental illness, social media and social isolation, as there have been a few suicides recorded recently in that community.

Chapter 12

DEPRESSION AND SUICIDE

Did you know that majority of people who die by suicide don't have clinically diagnosed depression, or other mental illness for that matter? Yeah, I know, I felt the same way when I learned about it myself. Now, let me explain. The route to suicide is strewn with a combination of despair, hopelessness, helplessness and eventually, deep depression. Note that the depression often comes at the end, the consequence of life's travails, or as a complication of life's trauma. As one blogger described it, suicide is the *"ultimate state of human burnout."* The victim often feels like they have run out of options and becomes emotionally and mentally exhausted. However, there are many factors in our day to day life that lead to suicidal ideations, not only depression. Financial issues, relationship failures, chronic illness, major trauma, loss of a loved one, family history of suicide, access to firearms, business failure etc. are some factors that can trigger suicidal thoughts and behavior. One must be cognizant of that fact, so we don't inadvertently treat everyone for *"depression"* with antidepressants.

Over time we have been made to believe that 80-90% of people who die by suicide have clinical depression. In other words, depression is often blamed for most suicides. If that is the case, with the quadrupling of antidepressant prescriptions in the US, why then are suicide rates still at an all-time high, and climbing? Are we over diagnosing depression? Are we looking for underlying causes? Are we peeling off all the layers? Should we be? Are we settling for an *"easy low hanging fruit"* called depression? Thankfully, there are studies that have refuted that thought process, and we are now discovering that in truth, nearly 90% of people who have (appropriately diagnosed and treated) clinical depression *do not* die by suicide.

Rather, less than half, 46% of suicides according to National Alliance on Mental Illness (NAMI) have been shown to have a diagnosis of mental illness at the time of death.

What I will say therefore, is that untreated mental illness, inability to cope with life's stresses, lack of adequate support from family members and medical providers, a multiplicity of other factors coupled with a genetic predisposition can lead to suicide. This is so important to know because as aforementioned, quite often, the stigma of mental illness and the shame and embarrassment over life's ups and downs do prevent people from reaching out for help. Teenagers are at a particularly vulnerable age; they generally don't want to share much with adults for fear

47

of judgement. They prefer to share with their peers who are often not much more knowledgeable than they are. Since their brains are still developing, it is often a critical time for them, so, *knowing, acknowledging and validating* their emotions is a very important protective factor against suicide in teens.

Chapter 13

THAT DAY IN SAN FRANCISCO

The entire excessive cellphone / device use thing reminds me of an incident that I experienced during Labor Day weekend of 2017 while visiting my son at Stanford University. I usually wake up each morning and go running. That morning, while exploring the neighborhood, I approached a bus stop, as I ran past, I counted a total of 13 people of mixed ages and races, each had their head bowed looking down at a handheld device. Not one of them looked up as I ran by, not one of them acknowledged the other who stood by, not one of them made eye contact or spoke a word. That image is still fixed in my head. The sight struck me as a sad one, because I realized that each person standing there, waiting for that bus, most likely came there each morning as they went about their business. They have possibly never once looked at each other or said a word to each other. None could probably describe the other's facial features, eye color or what they wear, yet, they all wait together at the same bus stop, day in and day out. What a sad state of affairs. We don't talk to each other anymore. Unfortunately, that is the situation everywhere: at bus stops, at school, at the airports, at the mall, and even at home! Very isolating, we are all very isolated. Look around you next time you are at the bus stop or airport, what do you see? Are my observations correct?

Now, close your eyes for a moment with me. Imagine that one of those people at that bus stop is a young girl struggling with depression or suicidal ideation for whatever reason. Imagine she woke up that morning and planned to end her life that day. Imagine that was her last bus ride. What if she stood at that bus stop wishing and waiting for someone to lift their eyes up and look at her, really see her. Maybe offer a kind word, a smile, a friendly nod, a hello. Any human gesture to make her feel like she exists, like she matters, like she is visible, and no one does. Imagine the difference, if one of them simply said a word. While we don't know for sure that the encounter would change her mind, we don't know for sure that it wouldn't either. What we do know for sure is humans yearn for human interaction and that makes a huge difference.

On national bullying day this year, while strolling around my neighborhood, I came upon a group of middle school kids waiting for their school bus. I decided to speak to them about bullying. None of them saw me approaching. They each stood silently, eyes on their phones. As I got closer, not one of them noticed. I literally walked right into their faces and said hello before any of them looked up. Some appeared irked, a few were genuinely interested in what I had to say, and a couple didn't even bother to engage. I introduced myself and told them about the work that I do with at-risk teens. I then proceeded to give them a talk on bullying and its effect on suicide in school-aged kids. I talked about the need for more eye contact, more friendliness and kindness. The need for them to buddy up with each other, and what to do when they observe bullying going on. The session ended with a group hug and individual high fives. They had made my day, and I knew I had made theirs too because by the time their school bus arrived, they were hugging each other, high fiving each other, and wanting to get in a photograph with me 😊. I made each one promise to take a brief break from their phones from time to time and appreciate their surroundings, enjoy the outdoors and connect with each other. Children need to stay connected; we all do. We all need that sense of community.

Chapter 14

MS. BURKE AND THE #ME-TOO MOVEMENT

In 1997, when Ms. Tarana Burke (sitting across the table from a troubled teen) first uttered the words *"me too,"* she had absolutely no idea that those words would have a global impact two decades later. Nothing would have prepared her for the movement it has now become. What she was simply doing that day, was speaking out. Speaking up about her own rape and sexual molestation. In essence, she was saying NO MORE SILENCE! She was looking for the right words to identify with another female who had been sexually assaulted, a way to connect with another human being who had been broken. She refused to believe that shame and stigma were her only options. She was saying no more silence to sexual assault and the guilt that comes with it. She was saying the silence must end. She talked to anyone who would listen. She shared her story, her pain, her suffering. She was going to speak about it no matter what, because *she* was the victim, and *she* knew that true healing would only come when *she* began to *talk* about it.

Today, the *#metoo* movement is a worldwide phenomenon that is bringing awareness to the menace of sexual assault in our communities. It is helping to bring some degree of closure for victims who have suffered far too long in silence. Victims are now able to identify with each other, knowing that a problem shared is a problem halved. In Michelle Obama's words, *"together we are stronger."* And though the stigma and shame still exist around sexual assault in the world, there is light at the end of the tunnel (albeit dim).

I suggest we take a leaf from Ms. Burke and start to talk about our struggles with mental illness. Stop keeping it a secret. It is said that secrets are often destructive. I say secrets are not only destructive, they can also lead to death, suicide death that is. Thankfully, not only is depression completely treatable, suicide is also *almost* completely preventable.

Ending the silence, stigma and shame is my hope for depression and suicide. Talking about it is also my primary M.O. What about you? Will you do the same? Will you join me in spreading awareness for depression and suicide? Will you add your voice in saying #metoo, and stand up for those of us suffering with mental illness? Will you join us in saying *"enough is enough"* to the silence? Will you resist the status quo and stop stigmatizing suicide? If we each vowed to make a difference in our own little corners of the world, it is only a matter of time before the dim light at the end of the tunnel becomes a flood light, and we are all able to light up the world and extinguish the darkness of despair and depression and suicide. After reading this book, I hope you find it in your heart to join the movement.

Part 2

Faces, Fears, Fights

"I wanted to live; I just didn't know how to anymore."

~ Shelby Rowe

Chapter 15

SEXUAL ASSAULT AND CUTTING

"The silence was killing me. And that's all there was. Silence. It was all I knew. Keep quiet. Pretend nothing had happened, and nothing was wrong. And look how well that was turning out."

~ J. Lynn

Abigail

Hi Doctor Lulu,

I am sitting on the edge of my bathtub, with a razor blade in my right hand, trying to contemplate my next move. I hesitate and look up, catching the reflection of my face on my oval mirror, I am hardly able to recognize myself. I feel bad, really bad. How did I get to this point? This is my lowest point ever. I have no idea how I ended up here. Unhappy, sad, depressed and suicidal. How?

I am a high school senior. My family is originally from the Netherlands, but my great-grandparents emigrated to the United States in the early 20s. I really don't like talking about myself. I never want any extra attention drawn to me, but I guess at this point I must. I feel like my depression, feelings of worthlessness, sadness, anxiety, sleeplessness, decreased energy, and feeling like I am alone in the world, are all *mine*, and I would rather not share them with anyone. I have always felt alone in this world, like no one can see me, no one can hear me, like I am unseen… I am very shy and reserved and like

57

to remain invisible. I have come to enjoy staying in my own little corner. This way, no one will miss me when I'm gone.

Most times I feel like I have been betrayed by my family. My parents split up before I was born, they went their separate ways and basically leave me to fend for myself for the most part. I tell myself it is because they are busy with work, which is mostly true. I live with my mom, Anne. I get to see my dad every other weekend. I live for those weekends with my dad, so I don't have to deal with my mom and her friends who don't understand me. They think I am spoiled and incorrigible, just so you know, the feeling is mutual.

My mom works as a hospital administrator, so she can afford to buy me anything I want, which is cool, but because she travels a lot on business for her job, my payback is leaving me with extended family most of the time. At 17 years old, I can stay at home alone, but my mom will not hear of it. So, it's either I stay with my Aunt Suzanne, or my uncle Jamie. Since Aunt Suzanne is now dating and mostly busy with her new boyfriend, it is almost always Uncle Jamie, and he insists on coming over to the house to house-sit and babysit me, and that is the problem.

The last time he came over, he tried to come into my bedroom, again. Since I know his routine, I often pack up enough food and snacks into my closet and dresser before he arrives, and I lock myself in my room until my mom gets back. I decided enough is enough the last time he cornered me while my mom was in the house! Next time he does that again will be the last. This entire thing with him goes back to my childhood years. I used to *love* to spend time with him.

He would take me to the park or to the greenway. When he attended the nearby community college, he would even take me to school with him to hang out with his friends. It was all fun and games when I was between the ages of 3 and 10 years old, but then came puberty and adolescence and, my breasts.

Ugh! Those early days when my breasts were developing were awful! It was bad enough that they hurt, all the time, but uncle Jamie also took notice of them and started to make silly comments. He would say gross stuff like, *"Wow, our little Abbey is becoming a lady,"* or *"Ab, I see your little tree has borne fruits.* I hated it when he talked like that. My mom would find it weirdly funny and laugh about it. She never knew how much his words hurt. But then again, I never told her. Then he started treating me differently. He would act out his feelings, becoming more vocal and daring and making me even more self-conscious. I began to feel more and more uncomfortable around him. Since my mom always sides with her brother, I hadn't bothered to tell her in the beginning, because I knew she would not believe me, and now, I think it might be too late. Even if she believes me now, I don't think it would be worth it, I don't want to deal with the embarrassment of telling her and risk her not believing me, or things possibly getting out of hand with my uncle, because she might tell him.

The first time I realized my uncle was acting a bit different was one time he faked an accidental brush against my blouse to touch my breasts. He pretended to wipe something off my t-shirt. I initially told myself it must have been an accident, but I have now noticed him doing inappropriate stuff like that more and more often. For instance, he always wants me to sit next to him during family movie nights, or he would come outdoors when I retreat to my swing-set for some quiet time, and sit on the empty swing next to me, smiling sheepishly, never taking his eyes off my breasts.

I know this is really bad, and I want to tell someone. But my mom will never listen. She will take sides with her brother as always and I don't want to deal with that any longer. My dad would probably put a bullet in his chest if he ever caught wind of it, and as much as I want to tell him, I can't bring myself to do it. I also don't want this to get out, so, I haven't told any of my friends in school. The last time I tried to tell them, they thought it was funny and started to tease me about it, so I have chosen to tell no one, and do my best to avoid him as much as I can. These days, I feign abdominal pains and stay home most weekends my mom goes to visit my grandma because he lives there. I love my grandma dearly, but I feel trapped and would rather stay home than go anywhere near him.

Three days ago, while I was walking home from school, his car suddenly appeared from nowhere, and drove up to me, I hastened up my footsteps and tried my best to walk away as fast as possible. I refused to get in the car when he persisted and increased his speed, I freaked out and ran as fast as I could all the way home. Thankfully my mom was there. I ran into the house and ran straight to my room and locked the door. Can you believe that my mom didn't even notice anything? She never asked me what was going on or why I ran straight to my room. My uncle came in the house and it was business as usual... I HATE THAT! She doesn't see me!

Unfortunately, earlier this afternoon, my luck ran out. My mom had to step out for a minute, leaving the two of us alone in the house. Before I could go into my room and lock the door, he was on top of me. He pushed me against the doorway and tried to kiss me. I could smell his nasty breath all over my face...All my neck hairs stood on end. I was so afraid. I wasn't sure that screaming would help. So, I started pleading with him to leave me alone. I threatened to tell my mom this time if he hurt me. I screamed at the top of my lungs, but no one was in sight, no one heard. We were all alone in the house. He laughed his wicked laugh at me, and smirked, breathing heavily down my neck. As insane luck would have it, as soon as he started pulling at my blouse and tugging at my skirt, the garage doors opened, my mom was home.

I finally decided to tell my mom while we were eating dinner tonight. I told her everything, that my uncle was coming on to me. I told her how he looks at me with lust in his eyes, and how he tried to push me into my room the one day, how he was the reason I ran home the other day. I told her about this afternoon, I told her how helpless and trapped he makes me feel in my own home. I begged her to please allow me to stay home alone, I don't need a babysitter. Can you believe that it backfired? My mom was livid! She accused me of being ungrateful. Called me a brat and went on to tell me how my uncle has been there for me my whole life, even when my father hadn't. She reminded me of the time I had gotten sick with a strange

61

illness at 8 years old. How he would come and spend the entire day with me in the hospital when neither she nor my dad was able to be there due to work. Even though I was sick, that memory still makes me shudder. I still smell his cologne mixed with sweat, the same nasty mix of smells every day. I remember him getting in the hospital bed and slowly rubbing his hands up and down my thigh repeatedly, telling me I was going to be fine. *"Uncle will take care of you."* I hated it so much. I wanted to scream and ask him to go away, but the nurses would come by and praise him, telling me how lucky I was to have such a doting uncle!

This reminds me of one time when I was 12 years old and my mom had had some friends and family over. It was late in the night, I had school the next day, and I was trying to get to sleep. I heard the knock on my door, but didn't respond, I needed to sleep. My uncle came into my bedroom any way, he mumbled that he was *"looking for something."* He walked into the room and hovered by the bed next to me. I pretended to be asleep, but I heard him, and smelled him. He probably thought I was asleep, but I was fully awake. I felt his presence even before I saw him walk up to me. After a brief hesitation, he bent over and touched me ever so lightly whispering something I couldn't quite make out due to the noise from the party in the house. I saw him slowly slide his left hand into his jean pants, and slowly started caressing himself. Then he sat on the bed and started stroking my shins, first over the blanket, then he lifted the blanket off and touched my skin... I stiffened and froze and held my breath as he slowly moved his hand up to my knees on his way to my thighs. Thankfully I heard my mom call out to him, which made him stop, and stare blankly at me just a little longer. Even in the dark, I could feel the wicked grin in his eyes as he slowly turned around and headed out the door. As soon as the door closed shut, I jumped off my bed, ran over and locked it! Only then did I finally exhale and shakily walked back to my bed, clutched my bedcover closer, and cried myself to sleep. I hate my uncle!

I started cutting the next morning. I first heard about kids that cut a few years ago in my school. I had always thought of them as weirdos. Never thought I would one day be confessing to doing the same thing. I remember walking into my bathroom that morning, I looked at my face in the mirror and all I could feel was repulsion and disgust. I hated, and still hate looking at myself! I felt like I was the only person in this world. *I felt ugly.* As I reached over to pick out a scrunchie for my hair, my eyes caught a pack of beautiful disposable razors my mom had bought me from one of her trips to Bali. I had never opened them. I hesitated, then I reached for the pack. It was like an out of body experience, I saw myself open the pack and pull one out. Each one had a beautiful floral design on it, tiny little ringlets of pink flowers... So beautiful. It looked so sharp, so shiny, so... Then it happened all too quickly, I placed a tiny (almost cute) superficial transverse cut on my right thigh. It hurt. It hurt a lot. It felt good. It bled. It bled a lot. That first cut was... I let the blood trickle out for what seemed to be a long minute before placing paper-towel over the area. I closed my eyes and savored the pain.

At first, it was an experiment of sorts. I told myself I would only do it that one time, but now I am realizing it is a place I like to go to help me cope, to help me feel, to help me be. Luckily, I have a lot of skin, my wrists, my chest, abdomen, breasts, even pubic area. The pain is good punishment. I deserve it. I like it. A good kind of pain. It helps me deal with the feelings of self-hatred that come from helplessness and unwanted attention from close male family members. From a mother who does not understand, from a father who is not present, from friends who don't get it... from everyone. Yes, I now enjoy cutting. I can't explain why I do, but I find that I even crave it sometimes. My cuts are tiny. They are all over the place. The scars are my warrior lines. They are mine, not to share with anyone. So, I wear long sleeves almost every day, because I am determined to hide them from everyone.

Every so often I find my left radial pulse and place right forefinger and middle finger over it, close my eyes and wonder, what if... I have a lot of razors, they are all sharp. It will hurt, but it will also happen very quickly, I think. But the pain will stop. All of it will stop.

Abby.

Dear Abby,

Thank you so much for sharing your story with me, with us, with the world. I know first-hand how difficult sharing that kind of truth can be. I was molested as a child myself, though it wasn't a family member, it was however someone I knew. I had a very hard time talking about

64

it, and it took most of my life to tell my parents. As you may or may not know, many victims of sexual abuse are unable to come forward with it, so again, I applaud you for coming forth with yours.

I am sorry you found yourself in such a difficult place in your life that you felt self-harm was an effective coping mechanism. You remind me of a patient I once had who had cuts all over her anterior abdomen and no one knew until the day I discovered them during a physical examination, to the surprise of everyone in the room.

Thankfully, treatment is available. It entails different forms of therapy (discussed below) designed to help you manage your emotions, learn self-care, self-compassion, self-kindness and self-forgiveness. You will get better. It might just take time. But for that to happen, you will have to be prepared to include your parents in the process, for support, for all its worth. I know that might be difficult for you, but it would eventually be the best path to follow for everyone concerned. The first order of business would be to remove your uncle from your immediate environment, indefinitely. I personally think he should be charged with sexual assault as soon as possible, because many times molesters have multiple victims.

If you could begin by telling your parents everything, that might make things a little easier for you. Maybe request a meeting with the two of them, together. Your parents love you and will understand and get you the best kind of help. I am sorry about your experience with your mom, but I know she still loves you. Sometimes people react in unpredictable ways out of fear and uncertainty. She might have been uncomfortable with talking about it with you directly. She too, might have been a victim of sexual trauma, who knows. I would never make excuses for her behavior, all I am saying is let's try again, this time, with your father in the room.

Family therapy will hopefully teach them the proper way to be supportive of you. I will also help you come up with an appropriate long-term plan that will put you on the road to recovery.

Again, thank you for sharing your story with me, I am sorry for all you have had to endure at such a young age. Betrayal from family and friends is always the worst kind. My hope is you find answers, peace and healing, and I hope your pain truly stops, but the right way.

Yours in healing,
Dr. Lulu.

Discussion

Studies show that most perpetrators of child sexual abuse are people known to the victims. In the US, up to 90% of victims know their abusers, and 30% of these victims are abused by family members. Unfortunately, for many reasons like Abby noted: disbelief by the family, distrust of the family, victim-blaming, fear of repercussion from the perpetrators and shame and guilt prevent many victims from coming forward, further worsening the stigma. And without a safe place to go, some might then look for other avenues to cope and deal with it.

Cutting is a form of self-harm or NSSI (see above). It is defined as the act of deliberately hurting oneself with a sharp object-enough to break the skin and make it bleed. It usually starts in teenage years and can last into adulthood. Cutters often hide their cuts and scars, hence many of them wear long sleeves even in the hot summer. Like Abby, the commonest areas are on the wrists, thighs, anterior abdominal walls, inside the upper arm or anterior chest wall. Other forms of self-harm include burning the skin with cigarette lighters or match sticks, extinguishing cigarettes on the skin, hitting or bruising of oneself, extreme skin picking or scratching, or deliberately breaking a bone.

These individuals are often ashamed of the behavior, they hide the scars, and engage in the act in secret, when they are alone. Sufferers say they get relief from the bad feelings when they engage in the behavior. They report that it helps them numb the emotional pain they are going through. Some see it as a form of self-punishment and the endorphins released during the tissue injury brings a calming effect and emotional relief.

Sexual assault along with bullying or belonging to the LGBTQ community are the top risk factors for self-harm. While self-harm often induces, pain, survivors of abuse or stress maintain that it helps relieve their pain and helps them get control of it. Though the behavior can often coexist with other mental health diagnoses like depression, obsessive compulsive disorder, anxiety or bipolar disorder, it often occurs on its own.

Self-harm is largely treatable, but the first step is to tell someone about it, so they can get help. Treatment will be based on their specific issues and any related mental health disorders they might have. Because self-injury can become a major part of their life, it's best to get treatment from a mental health professional experienced in self-injury issues for the long-term. The process will involve going to see a doctor for a full physical and psychological examination, and a referral to an appropriate specialist. Scars are generally diagnostic of the behavior.

For treatment, Dialectical Behavior Therapy (DBT), or Cognitive Behavior Therapy for Suicide Prevention (CBT-SP) are forms of therapy which teach coping skills, risk reduction, relapse prevention all targeted towards suicidal, depressed youth. They help patients identify and manage the underlying issues that trigger self-injuring behavior. Collectively, they will help with the following:

- Learn skills to better manage distress
- Learn how to regulate their emotions
- Learn how to boost their self-image
- Develop skills to improve their relationships and social skills
- Develop healthy problem-solving skills

For effective treatment, removal from the stressful environment, proper care of wounds resulting from cutting and any other necessary lifestyle changes are included.

Lastly, in the US, the hotline for self-harm is 1-800-DONTCUT or 1-800-366-8288, and sexual assault help is available at 800-656-HOPE and online.rainn.org.

Chapter 16

BETRAYAL AND ALCOHOL USE DISORDER

"I wish all teenagers can filter through songs instead of turning to drugs and alcohol."

~ Taylor Swift

Meagan

Hi doctor Lulu, how are you doing? My name is Meagan, but everyone calls me Meg. Though my name means *"I am beautiful"* these past few months have given me nothing to feel beautiful about. I am currently in 12th grade and am not currently doing too well academically. I do plan on going to college next year, but I haven't really started applying. I have been putting it off to worry about the issues that have arisen in recent times that involved a lot of betrayal from people I thought were my friends.

I broke up with my boyfriend Michael, last year. And even though I tell myself that I have moved along (because I have), I am still very mad at him and my best friend, Lisa for what they did

69

behind my back. I thought she was a good friend. I thought she had my back. I thought he was a good guy. He was my first boyfriend for *gossake!* I even thought I loved him. I was wrong big time, frankly I think they deserve each other.

My *"best friend"* did the unthinkable. She stole my boyfriend! The bad thing is, I trusted the two of them with my deepest secrets, my deepest thoughts. Lisa and I have been friends since elementary school. We had been inseparable since we first met after she and her family moved next door to my grandmother's house. We did everything together, dance recitals, ballet lessons, girl scouts... everything. Last summer, however, while she was visiting her grandparents in Seattle, I convinced my parents to allow me to sign up for a swim camp, and that was where I met Michael. He was a lifeguard at the pool. He had just transferred this school year to our school from another school district. We discovered we had a lot in common. We shared some mutual friends, but because we went to different high schools, I had never met him before. That was the best summer ever. Michael and I instantly became inseparable, and that helped me through the summer without Lisa. I told her all about him during our nightly girlfriend chats on the phone. I described everything in detail including our first kiss. Somehow, she never warmed up to any of the stories I told her about me and him. She kept finding reasons to put a damper on the relationship. At one point I even teased her that she was jealous of the two of us and told her that was completely understandable, but she denied it.

When school finally started back, I could not wait to introduce them to each other, and now I wish I never did, that first day of school. Hmmm! The worst part is at the very beginning, she tried to *"advise"* me to break up with him. She wanted me to leave him. She told me he wasn't good looking enough, not tall enough, not smart enough, and generally not fit to date me. She even gave me reasons why I'd be better off without him, that I can do so much better than him. She told me she had seen on some social media site that he is a playboy who has tried to be with every girl in his former school. The funny thing is she eventually got to me, and I ended up believing her, and I started looking for a reason to break up with him. When you have a bestie who you trust, you find yourself doing certain things even if you know better and don't really want to. Why? Why do folks do that, and why do we allow them to?

Michael himself, also tried to convince me that Lisa was mean and ugly. I wouldn't say he tried as hard as she did, but he would sometimes ask me why I was friends with her, that she looks mean and acts mean. I just wish he hadn't lied to me. You know? Pretending to dislike her, even to the point of trying to get me to stop hanging out with her. I am so mad at him! Ugh! The nerve! You want to know why I broke up with him? I had gone to the movie theater with my little sister one fateful evening, and as we were walking across the parking lot, I saw the two of them walking hand in hand out of the theater! I still can't believe how gullible I was! She had told me she hadn't been feeling well when I had asked her to go to the movies earlier that day. I had to work the late shift the next day at my part time job, so I thought it would be fun to hang out for a bit that evening. Aarrgghh!!!

I decided to go with my sister. I only asked her because Michael errands to run for his mom that weekend. I still can't believe they would creep around with each other like that behind my back! They didn't even look up as they walked past me, all I could do was stand there, staring, unable to believe my eyes.

The worst part of this whole thing is I hadn't even wanted to start dating in the first place. And never thought I would ever fall for a guy like him... A mama's boy. There were lots of other boys wanting my attention, but I eventually went with Michael when he wouldn't stop pestering me and following me everywhere. In all fairness, he was funny and good looking in a boyish sort of way. He had a car (his old jalopy), and I loved the way he used it to help other people, like running errands for his mom. We had some good times in that car 😊

I thought he cared about me, or at least he did before my (supposed) best friend took him from me. Though he was never one to really show too much emotion, I still liked him, you know? He made me smile and made me forget about my stress. School is hard enough, so when I was with him, I enjoyed not having to worry about schoolwork. Truth be told, I kind of knew he had a reputation as a bad boy, but you know how when you like someone, you either refuse to see their bad traits, or you forgive them easily, or worse, you want them to change, and you hold out hope as long as you can... I hoped he would change *for* me. I hoped I could *love him right.* So, finding out that he was cheating on me, with none other than my own best friend? That was a deep cut, a deep stab in my back!

I know you understand why I am upset. Have you ever been heart-broken? Dr. Lulu? Ever had your boyfriend cheat on you before? No one wants to be taken advantage of or feel betrayed. That hurts a lot. And lying about it to me is just such a shame. Anyone else in my shoes would be equally upset and angry, and never want to see or speak to them again! I wish I had taken pictures of them that night, I could have exposed their lying cheating a**es on social media! So, I avoid her in school at all costs, because I honestly don't know what I would do to her if our paths cross again, I have already unfriended the two of them, and blocked them on all my apps. I don't want to get in a fight and possibly get expelled from school this close to graduation, but, it's oh so tempting!

In the past several months, I have found myself some new friends. They are fun to hang out with. They meet after school and go to the neighborhood pool for snacks and to just chill out. These are kids I would never have hung out with in the past, but now I realize they are not so bad to be around. A couple of them even smoke weed and drink alcohol and generally get high. This one girl brought some Xanax pills to school one time. She said it belonged to her mom. She wanted me to try one, she said it would make me feel better. I hesitated at first, but then I was like, *"why da heck not?"* So, I tried a couple of them. They weren't too bad. Shhh, my mom would kill me if she ever found out.

It all started as a trial. A classmate, Ryan (one of the new kids I hang out with) has always liked me. After the breakup he saw how bad I was feeling and offered me a shoulder to lean on. I know he has had a crush on me, but I was hurting so much I went along with him for the ride. At that point, I had nothing to lose. Plus, I am single… He was the first to offer me alcohol and weed, told me all the other kids were into it. He assured me that the weed was not laced. The days and weekends with Ryan and my new friends have been crazy. You see, it was only supposed to be one time. One quick taste, a *"see-if-you-like-it"* type thing. At first, I hated it, the taste of alcohol was disgusting. The smoke of the fumes where choking… Furthermore, I was afraid that I would get drunk, or get too high and my mom would smell it on me... But eventually, over the next few days and weeks, I began to get used to the tastes. The more I drank, the better it tasted. The more I smoked, the better I felt. It dulled my senses, and slowed everything down in my head, so I didn't have to worry about the pain in my heart. I stopped eating as well and as healthy as I used to, and my diet has sucked. I have been eating mostly junk and not as hungry as I used to be when I got home from school. I felt bloated and fuzzy-headed a lot. I began to lose weight as a result, and overall not doing well. I never really wanted to start drinking. You know? Because I know better, but I also didn't want to be left out, I needed to show these guys that I could *"hang."*

I can't even believe I am the same person drinking and getting stoned. I wonder what Michael and Lisa would say if they knew what I have been up to recently… Who cares?!

Just last month, I had to get my fix so badly, but my new friends were nowhere to be found. I have no money, so for one moment, I actually considered stealing my mom's jewelry to sell for money! That to me was the lowest point. I couldn't believe that was me, this is me, thinking of stealing to furnish my habit. I didn't do it, but at this point I find myself preoccupied with getting a hit day in and day out. I hate it! I hate the feeling. The emptiness inside. I don't like it, but I don't quite know what to do about it.

I know this is not me though. This is not who I am… This is not the Meagan of my childhood dreams, the person I always wanted to be. This is not what I thought my teen years would be like or end up like. And to think that all of this is happening because I started dating. I should never have started dating, and I should never have allowed him to get into my head like he did. No one is worth throwing away my life for. Michael hurt me, Lisa did too. They both hurt me, badly, but Lisa, in addition to the hurt, disappointed and betrayed me. However, hurting myself and my body should not be the best way to get even, it's not even a way to do anything. I don't want to die. I don't want to become an alcoholic. I have an uncle who is an alcoholic, and I know the devastation first-hand. I know how he has left his wife and kids broke, and how he gambles with the kids' college funds to support his habit. I also hear alcoholism runs in the family, is that true Dr. Lulu? Will I become an alcoholic because my uncle is one?

It's been nearly 6months now since I started drinking. And Ryan has pretty much moved on with his friends, I guess I am not that much fun to be with now. So, I have no friends. I must fend for myself. I am beginning to experience sleepless nights, on a couple of occasions, I have gone days without sleep, and my face is beginning to show it. When my teachers ask me at school, I tell them I am up studying or doing my homework. I believe I am experiencing withdrawals. I never thought I would ever consider hurting myself, but I need to end this pain. No one knows about it at home. If they have noticed, they are not saying anything. I have seriously thought about overdosing on pills, but I don't have any.

I don't need help, so please don't suggest that. I need to end this pain inside. I can't tell anyone. I don't want to be a disappointment or a failure. I don't want to be a burden, and I certainly don't want to continue like this. I don't want to live anymore. It hurts too much. I remember one time we went to my uncle's house to visit I found his gun... I just need to find a reason to go over for a visit, and *"borrow it."* Thanks for taking the time to read my letter though. I appreciate it.

Meagan.

Dear Meagan,

I completely understand and empathize with you and your situation. Something similar happened to me when I was a little older than you. I know how hard it must be to lose a boyfriend and a best friend at the same time. The main question is, were they really your good friends to begin with? Life is full of ups and downs, and sometimes one must wonder why these things happen. It's so easy to get lost in the what ifs. But we must move on and forge ahead. This is only the beginning for you. You will get through this and you will rise and shine again. But we don't want to cause any lasting damage to your body while going through the motions. My concern is that it is only a matter of time before you start to experience worsening symptoms of drug or alcohol abuse.

And yes, alcoholism does have a genetic component. Among those abusing alcohol, people who are genetically predisposed to alcoholism have a higher risk of developing an alcohol use disorder or addiction. Although people can inherit alcoholic tendencies, the development of an alcohol use disorder is also dependent on social and environmental factors. An environmental stressor, such as a breakup in your case, is a common risk factor for alcohol use disorder. In general, the more risk factors a person has, the greater the chance of developing addiction.

My advice is for you to seek help as soon as you can. Are there any immediate or extended family members you can speak to about this in confidence? Do you have someone you can trust at school? Your guidance counselor or one of your school nurses or teachers? In the worst-case scenario, here is a number you can call for help in the meantime it is the national drug abuse hotline, 1-800-662-HELP (4357). There are also loads of websites and apps you can use to get help, a simple google search would be a good start. It might entail going to a rehabilitation facility, and possibly experiencing withdrawals, because you might need a detoxification process. Either way, be prepared for the worst to happen before the good will follow.

I think the fact that you have some degree of insight and awareness of the gravity of the problem is a good thing. Stay away from any thoughts of self-harm. Please remove all thoughts of getting your uncle's gun from your mind. That is the most dangerous move you could ever make. I know all sorts of havoc a gun in the home can cause firsthand, and we definitely don't want to go there.

I would like to add, that you might need to find new friends. I know that can be relatively difficult. The problem is, when you find a group of people that you feel a connection with, but they turn out to be a negative influence, then you must cease and desist from hanging out with them as a matter of urgency and necessity. I know like most teens you feel a need to have friends and people to hang out with, but we must first get you clean and sober. Once you are at a good/better place emotionally, then the good friends will come. You are a good friend and a great person. Unfortunately, I wish I could promise you that people like Michael and Lisa don't exist, but they do. Let's get you some help first, everything else will fall in its proper place…with time. You do have your whole life ahead of you, but let's focus on getting you better first.

We must also worry about your future with regards to college plans. If you do plan on going to college, then we must get you to a more stable emotional state. College is going to come with its own challenges, and we must be prepared for them. I remember you saying you hadn't started applying yet, maybe it is time to start doing something about that.

I wish you all the very best though. Let me know if you need anything, or if there is some other way I can help. Always remember that you come first, your feelings come first, and your heart comes first☺.

Yours in recovery,
Dr. Lulu.

Discussion

Did you know that substance abuse in teens is a growing epidemic worldwide? Recent research has shown that teenagers, much like Megan abuse <u>alcohol</u> more than any other substance in the United States. 11% of all the alcohol consumed in the US is by kids her age (11-20 years), 11% is about 1 in 10, right? That's a lot of kids! As she experienced and bravely stated, many of these teens also engage in binge drinking and mixing of drinks with other substances. Unfortunately, that can increase risky behaviors. Binge drinking can lead to acute_alcohol poisoning which could have deadly outcomes. Many teens turn to drugs and alcohol in response to peer pressure or stress. Most of this begins as experimentation in high school, sometimes earlier. Some teenagers use drugs as self-medication to *"help with painful emotions,"* some are simply curious, and some are pressured to join the crowd often in a hope to get popular. Some have situations like Belinda's, where they have been hurt and have no way to cope, and their friends offer them *"a way out."*

Alcohol, much like Tobacco and Marijuana is a *"gateway drug,"* meaning, it often leads to the use of other addictive substances like: Vicodin, Opiates, LSD, Cocaine etc. Unfortunately, alcohol is 100% legal in the United States, and it is easily available to our children. Most of these are often consumed together at parties and get togethers. My concern for Megan is the potential for progression from alcohol to any of these other substances, and the consequences can be deadly.

Teens who drink alcohol or use drugs are at increased risk for alcohol-related problems like poor school performance, more substance abuse, delinquency and engaging in sexual activity. Sexual activity might increase the chances of teen pregnancy and sexually transmitted infections. Sadly, most kids don't know that alcohol abuse in high school impacts the brain just as hard as other drugs, therefore, memory problems and other lifelong brain issues are common. And with plans to go to college, that might create another problem for them.

Substance abuse in general, nearly always complicates any situation. Majority of depressed persons turn to alcohol or other substances for solace. This often affects their mental health and decision-making capabilities further worsening an already bad situation. Substance abuse is not only a symptom but can also exacerbate suicidal behavior (discussed in part 3 of this book), so it must be discouraged and discontinued at all costs, especially in teens.

Chapter 17

BULLYING AND SUICIDAL IDEATION

"You can't be against bullying without actually doing something about it".

~ Randi Weingarten

Marisa

To Whoever Finds This Letter

By the time you find this, I will most likely no longer be alive. I will be gone. That is the only way the bullying will stop. I already have a plan and you can't stop me. There is no use hanging on, hoping the meanness will stop. I am tired of being bullied. For most of my life, I have been the victim of bullies. I have always been the odd one out, so, it's been easy to be the butt of most of the mean jokes. I have endured the bullying for years and years now, but I don't have to anymore. I am writing this to tell someone out there that there is a way out of the pain and suffering, and this is my way. I don't have to continue to carry that burden. I have tried every avenue to help myself. I tried ignoring the bullies, but it did not work. If you have ever been bullied, you might know and understand what I am talking about. Even if you don't, I can't handle it anymore. You might not understand what it means to feel all alone in the world, to be visible only to bullies, and to be invisible to everyone else, but I do.

As early as I can remember from when I was in elementary school. I have been ridiculed by kids. On the school bus, in the playground, on the way home, in the school hallways, in the bathrooms, everywhere I went. I was laughed at and I was teased almost daily. I remember how helpless I felt, how hard it was for me to get on the school bus every day. I did nothing to deserve that kind of treatment. My only crime was that my father was, and still is a migrant farmer. As a result of his type of work, we move a lot. I have attended a different school every 3 years or so. I have always been the new kid in the neighborhood, the new kid on the bus, the new kid in the classroom.

The worst time of all was in the 6th grade when the kids were particularly mean to me. They made up rumors about me and my family, some would say we were homeless. Some would say we eat out of the trash, or we bought our clothes at Goodwill. Yes, my family struggled financially. We were too poor to buy new clothes, most of the time we wore hand-me-downs, and we did shop at Goodwill a lot, but that was not my choice. I used to hate going shopping for clothes there. I would always pray never to run into any of my classmates. Unfortunately, it happened, a lot.

When I got to middle school, this one girl took it upon herself to be my personal bully. It started from the very first day I got to that school. She made up a song about me. She would make fun of my clothes, my shoes, my hair, my book bag, everything! She was also much bigger than me and much bigger than most of the kids in our grade, so, many of the kids were afraid of her and did as she asked. They would join her in chanting about me everywhere I went. It. Was. Terrible! This happened every day for months! I HATED getting on that school bus and going to school ☹. Sadly, no one ever came to my aid or cared how I felt or thought to stop them. Not one of those kids ever really *saw* me. They looked at my face, but they never saw me.

As bad as bullying in middle school was, nothing could have prepared me for high school. Now in high school, it is a different kind of bullying. No one speaks to me, ever. Not even when we are in groups for our class projects. When they are addressing me, they don't look me in the eye, sometimes, they don't even look in my direction. Everyone is so divided; the girls all walk around in clicks based on their race. The White girls hang out together. The Black girls do the same. The few Hispanic girls in my grade either don't see me at all or pretend not to. I am all alone. Thankfully, I will attend the same high school until I graduate. In that regard, I have had some semblance of normalcy, but I still have no friends.

One other thing, I have never felt beautiful. I have always been self-conscious about my acne and my weight. Two things I can't help but have, due to my adolescence. My mom and I are shaped the exact same way. She tries to tell me I should look beyond the physical appearance and know that I have a good heart, but that is so hard. I hate being overweight! I hate not having any friends. I am 17 and not dating. All the other girls have boyfriends already... I hate my life!

The worst part is that my mom and I hardly get along. She was born and raised in Mexico. She has a traditional Mexican mindset. She believes that I am overly Americanized, and she has a hard time understanding my issues. So, she often tells me to get over it whenever I try to confide in her. She does not approve of my mood swings and believes I am somehow weak and wimpy. I wish she understood me better, at least I would find some respite at home, but she doesn't, and my father is barely home. When my *"abuela"* was alive, things were a bit better, she would hug me and brush my hair and tell me everything would be okay. Now my mom just tells me to grow up and be a good example as a big sister to my siblings. That is so tough for me.

I heard that journaling is supposed to help with coping with my emotions. But it has not helped me so far. Very recently, the teasing has now gone online. The mean girls now send nasty messages. I don't even know how they got my information. They post mean stuff about me online. I receive anonymous text messages calling me names, telling me to get lost, and never return to school. I don't understand their motivation, I stick to myself. I don't have anything they should be jealous of. I hardly speak to any of them, yet they pick on me every chance they get.

I do think about my family sometimes. I wonder if they are going to miss me when I am gone. I know my mom loves me. I just wish she would show it a bit more. I know my dad loves me very much, but he is never home. I know my siblings: Elsa, Emmanuel and Annabella, do too, but I don't think this life is worth living. I can't get a break at school. Please tell my family that I love them. I will see them on the other side.

Dr. Lulu, if you are reading this, then I know as a doctor, you probably wouldn't advise me to hurt myself in anyway, but you are not walking in my shoes and you don't know what it is like to be me. I hear in the news and read on social media about kids that kill themselves, and I wish to join them. Besides, my aunt Stephanie had attempted suicide once when she was a teenager, and even though we don't talk about it much, I know about it. She is a hero in my book, but she did not complete it. I will complete it.

Marisa.

My dear girl,

First off, I would like you to know how sorry I am to hear about all that you have gone through. Like you, I was severely bullied as a child in elementary school, and it mostly took place on the school bus. Like you, I had no idea what I had done to deserve it, I never aggravated them or caused them any trouble, but they chose to bully me. To date, I still don't even know how I survived those years, but I did. I never told my parents, I never told anyone. Like you, no one came to my aid either. It was terrible, but I survived it. It took everything in my power to get on that school bus every day. One thing I did do was perfect the act of blocking them out of my mind until I was numb. I told myself they were just words, that my bullies were not worthy of me. I told myself that I was better than them, smarter than them and prettier than them. Finally, one day, it ended, I was done with school, I graduated and went on to high school and it never happened again. But I know how hard it was for me, words cannot describe how sorry I am that you have had to endure this throughout your school years.

Another thing I did was, bury myself in schoolwork. I ensured that I excelled in school and got out of there as fast as I could, I ended up skipping a grade and left early to high school. Looking back though, I wish I had said something, or done something, anything, to stand up for myself. In fact, most adults that were bullied in childhood, tell me that is their one regret, not sticking up for themselves. I have since learned that the two most important words when bullying is going on are *"STOP IT."* That phrase can make a huge difference. Did you know that bullies are *"hurt people?"* Yes, most of them are hurting inside. They might be victims of bullying themselves. It still doesn't make bullying right, but my friend Vicki Fitch once told me that, *"hurt people who aren't heard, hurt other people,"* and I believe her whole heartedly. I say this because they might need help themselves, but because they can't get it, they take out their frustrations on other people.

I would not suggest you ignore them anymore though. It is time you started standing up for yourself, and it is time to tell a responsible adult like your parents or someone at school about it. This way you can begin to be more assertive and self-protective. And if worse comes to worst, then I suggest you FIGHT BACK! You could sign up for a self-defense class at school, that will help boost your confidence. But I would rather you fight back and the two of you go down together, than you hurt yourself, alone. Because the bullying might never stop. Trust me you've got this. Fighting back also tells the bully you should not be messed with. Furthermore, that will ward off other bullies, and before you know it, you will be known as the *"fight-back-kid"* ☺

In honesty though, we are losing too many of our kids to suicide because they are not fighting back. I know that a few people might not agree with me, but I would be really proud of my child if they got in trouble in school for *fighting back a bully and standing up for themselves* than not. At this point, we must do whatever it takes to stop the ever-worsening bullying streak. A doctor friend of mine actually did that on her first day in high school many years ago. She had been bullied for a very long time by the same girl. One day she had had enough, and she reached deep inside for strength and fought back. Even though she was very afraid, she fought back anyway, and for the rest of her high school years she was left alone. That's what I call courage in my book, doing it afraid.

I know you repeatedly complain about not having any friends, so let's try to make friends. You could walk up to kids you share classes with and speak to them. Introduce yourself. You didn't mention this, but I am thinking you might be a shy introverted kind of person, and that is ok. But we shall require you to come out of your comfort zone in order to self-protect. Whatever you do, don't hurt yourself. Please don't. Not for a bully. They are teens just like you, they are not better than you in any way. So, don't let them win. This too shall pass. I know it is hard to see past today or even tomorrow, but these things never last forever. I promise you that.

I would also like to plead with you to please stop listening to the other kind of bully. The one in your head that is validating all the bad stuff those kids are saying about you. It's only your mind telling you lies. Lies like *"you are not good enough," "you are not smart enough," "you are not pretty enough,"* or that *"you can't do something you have set your mind to do."*

I am here to tell you that:

- You ARE good enough
- You ARE beautiful enough
- You ARE brave enough
- You ARE smart enough
- You ARE just enough

Yes, you are. Don't let anyone tell you are not. The bully in your head has a great memory and is always ready to remind you of previous bad experiences, and since she lives in your head, she goes to bed with you and wakes up in the morning with you. She looks and acts just like you. You need to take your power back from her. Once you start talking back to her and telling her she is lying, and refusing to listen to the *not enough* chant in your head, only then can you begin the journey to healing and the internal strengthening that it will take to overcome the external bullies. You can also tell her to *stop it* when next she starts with her lies.

Remember, the bully (whether internal or external) wants to hurt you. They get their energy from the effect they have on you. They feed off your reaction, so don't give them the benefit.

Lastly, I think some emotional help through counseling would be a great idea. Ask your mom to make an appointment with your pediatrician to get you a referral for counseling. She could find a counselor for you, or she could ask your school counselor for help. Know that sometimes you might need to try several counselors before you find one that's right for you, so be patient with yourself. The right counselor will help you find new ways to handle your struggles. You might also try volunteering or joining a club in school (see part 3 of this book below).

Again, please don't hurt yourself. I sincerely hope this letter reaches you on time. Until I hear back from you, keep telling yourself, and keep believing you are good enough. I love you so much. Oh, and by the way, it is probably best if we leave all talk about a boyfriend alone for now. It is very important that you find yourself first before you can find anyone else. A boyfriend at this time will only complicate further, an already really complicated issue. I hope you understand that, and are willing to do the work, before you know it, you will be the most attractive girl in the room (both in and out) 😊.

Warm hugs always,

Dr. Lulu.

Discussion

For bullying to take place, we need three ingredients: a power imbalance, an intent to harm or intimidate, and it must be repetitive. Bullying of all kinds is extremely rampant these days. I feel like in the old days, it wasn't as common or as complex as it is today, but I might be wrong. What I do know though is that bullying of today's children and teens is taking more and more extreme forms. Some starting as early as preschool, and the outcomes in victims are also worse. More and more victims are resorting to self-harm to deal with their bullying, and unfortunately, too many kids are also losing their lives to suicide as a result.

When we think about bullying, we often think of a frail kid getting beaten up by a much bigger kid, as bystanders look on. This is only partially true. Sometimes the bully is a sibling, a friend, a parent, or even oneself. Most people don't realize that there are 2 forms of bullying, the internal and the external. Majority of folks only think about the external bullying, when someone other than yourself is out to get you. While that is true, the worst kind of bullying unfortunately, is the kind that is from within. That is the concept I am trying to explain to Marisa above.

One thing most people do is ignore bullies, thinking that they will eventually stop on their own, or leave them to find another victim. While a few do, most of them don't. And that is why victims must tell someone like their parents, a relative, a teacher, counselor or the principal. Parents should go as far as the school district, or the state, if the bullying is not stopped at the school level. I know of parents who have filed lawsuits against school districts. Sadly, those often happen after there has been a suicide death by the victim. Parents must follow up on bullying cases, never assume that your child is doing okay, don't wait to act when it is too late.

Bullying erodes self-esteem. It is becoming a common reason for suicidal behavior. Like I explained to Marisa, parents need to play a pivotal role at home, by raising kind and sensitive kids who don't bully others, and by fully supporting their children who are victims. If you suspect your child is a bully, this article on my blog might help you figure out what to do and how to help them. Parents must also instill resiliency at an early age and encourage their children to fight back if, and when needed. The alternative of suicide is simply *not* an alternative.

Suicidal ideation is up to 8 times more prevalent in Mexican American teens living in the United States than other races. Studies have shown that those who experience decreased connectedness and decreased communication in their homes or within their family units are most at risk. This fact is quite understandable. Teens generally tend to be stuck uniquely between childhood and adulthood, and while they yearn to be grown and act like adults, most of them still seek parental guidance and love, and nearly all of them seek validation of their thoughts and actions.

Hispanic teens of Mexican descent in America, are at a crossroads. They are often wedged between the need to fit in with their American peers and staying true to their Mexican roots. This often causes them to appear too *Americanized* to their more traditional *Mexicanized* parents (is that even a word?) This could result in clashes at home, leading to self-esteem issues, difficulties with cultural orientation, a perceived discrimination, or ethnic identity crisis.

For some Hispanic youth, acculturation, the process by which recent immigrants adopt cultural norms of their new country, is at the crux of the relationship between self-esteem and discrimination in these teens. This set up, coupled with physical absence of their parents from the home, or the inability to talk to their parents, leads to increased emotional distress, suicidal ideation and suicidal attempts, especially in females. And if the teen is already experiencing other forms of trauma like ostracization or bullying, that can be a set up for worsening suicidal ideation. Some studies have stated that as many as one in seven female Hispanic teens living in the United States will attempt suicide. They generally struggle with issues concerning their culture, access to health care, family dynamics, language barriers, and poverty.

As I alluded to above (in part one), the generational clashes are also prevalent in other immigrant communities (African, Asian etc.) However, the Hispanic community has had extensive studies done on them, and for them, the link to suicidal behavior has been established.

Chapter 18

ABSENT BLACK FATHER SYNDROME
AND TEENAGE CRIME

"Fathers have a unique and irreplaceable role in the lives of children."

~ George W. Bush

Damiko

Hello Dr. Lulu,

How are you doing ma'am? My name is Damiko, I have always considered myself an athlete first. I played basketball, football, baseball, and I ran track. I was an example of an American boy next door when it came to sports. I lived with both my parents and my younger sister until our dad left us suddenly to pursue *"other passions"* when I was three. My younger sister is the apple of my eye, as much as she aggravates me to no end, I still love her. I love that she's always said she wants to be like me when she grows up, even though I am not too certain that is a good plan these days. I made decent grades in school: not a straight A student, but not failing either. Most of my friends' parents tell me they wish they had a son like me. I am guessing it is the athletics thing, but it might also be because I generally mind my business and stay focused. I help my mom around the home and have never really gotten in trouble.

I remember when I was much younger, how much I dreamed about becoming a football player, a quarterback in the NFL. Growing up, I would practice and practice and practice some more, mostly with friends because my dad left when I was still very young. I never had that father figure to show me the ropes or play ball with me like I saw some of the fathers in my neighborhood, but I was okay with it. My friends and their dads never let me feel any different. The only times I felt my father's absence (which was rarely), was during events at school, like the occasional father and son breakfasts. But I got used to it and moved on.

I am good at what I do. The entire high school is proud of me. They have always been very supportive. My teachers and coaches have told me I am sure to get a football scholarship for college. I was hoping to attend an HBCU like Howard University. Since everything looks so good in my story so far, it will come to you as a shocker when I tell you that I am thinking of buying a gun to end my life, right?

Ever since my dad left, I've always felt protective towards my mother and my sister. As we've grown up, my sister has joined me, and we are both very committed to doing everything within our

96

means to protect and care for our mother. She only had one family member left, our uncle, who used to be the family helper, but he got into some trouble with the law a few years ago and ended up in jail. He did his time, and when he got out, rather than getting better, things took a turn for the worse. He simply wasn't the same anymore. His wife left him after he ended up making strings of poor choices. It seemed like he picked up one bad habit after the other, excessive drinking, drug addiction and petty burglary. His behavior got so bad that he eventually lost his parole status and was back in jail. I watched all that take a huge toll on my mother.

She has literally worked herself to the bone, holding 2 or 3 jobs at any one time for as long as I can remember. We are not rich by any means, we live in the projects, but we are wealthy in love, our home is kept warm, and our lights are always on. We have food on our plates and clothes on our backs. When I was younger, I vowed to myself that I would not allow her to suffer or want for anything when I grow up. That's the reason I've been dedicated to football as my way out of the projects and hard times.

Growing up, I have watched other boys in the neighborhood hustle, and I have watched some live a life of crime. Crimes ranging from dealing drugs, petty theft, to murder, rape or sexual assault. I had refused to be influenced by them, I wanted to go to school get a good education, play pro-football and hopefully buy a nice home for my mother in a nice upscale suburban neighborhood. I had always been a good well-behaved kid at school, and I knew that if I continued the way I was going, I was going to get good letters of recommendations from my teachers and coaches to help with the football scholarship at a college of my choice.

Everything was going great, until one day my mother returned home from work and told us that my uncle had been found hanging in his jail cell from an apparent suicide. Like I mentioned earlier, my mom and my uncle were very close, he was her only sibling. The news of his death was bad enough on my mom, but within weeks, she was laid off her day job at Sam's Club. She has worked at Sam's club for nearly 18yrs, and she was hoping to remain there and get a decent retirement. We were all devastated by the events that were taking place, but my mom took it really hard, and went into severe depression. With little or no money, we had a hard time getting her the proper medical care that she needed. I couldn't believe this was happening. And then we had to worry about the bills and the utilities, it would only be a matter of time before we received a notice to vacate the housing project. It was a very tough few weeks and months, my mom had earlier forbidden us to work, because she wanted me to focus on my football and academics, and my sister to focus on school and a budding modelling career.

However, I knew I had to do what I could to help my mom. I needed to help my family, I knew I could get a job, but I that would take too long. There were funeral arrangements for my uncle yet to be made, there were unpaid bills for the morgue where he was, there are bills for our utilities and rent, my mom's doctor's visits and medications, daily needs for my sister and I, and so on. I just had a lot of pressure overall to help until my mom's condition improved, or until she got another job.

I applied for jobs all around the neighborhood, since we don't own a car, and I couldn't go looking for jobs too far from the home. I also felt a need to be close to home, since my mom wasn't and isn't doing so well.

I was so desperate that I reached out to some of the kids in my neighborhood that I knew relate to dealers. I needed cash, fast! Every bone in my body told me not to get involved with them. But my family was looking at the possibility of eviction, with no money coming in from anywhere. The stress was much, and I didn't want my 15-year-old sister to feel any of. It was an easy deal. We were to deliver some goods to someone for quick cash, and all I had to do was drive the getaway car (yes, my uncle taught me how to drive). The day came, and I did my part, and everything went well, I got my pay off and was able to help the family with much needed cash for living and maintenance, but it didn't last long, life happens.

I hadn't planned on telling my sister the source of the cash to begin with, but she begged and pleaded and would not let up, so I told her I borrowed it from some of the parents in the neighborhood and she believed me. Naturally, she told my mother. Though my mom was grateful for the assistance, she *knew* I didn't have a real job, and the money didn't come from the right source, but she didn't say anything. I should have listened to that inner voice that told me not to do it. I should have paid attention to the fact that I have my whole life ahead of me. But since my mom didn't *really* ask where the money came from, it was ok, wasn't it? The next time around things did not go as planned, shots were fired, and someone got hurt.

Though no one died, the entire experience really scared me. The police got involved and it's not looking too good. We are currently out on bail, because one of the kids' dad was able to get us a plea deal. Next thing I know my coach calls me to the locker room to discuss the incident. He is telling me I am out of the team. The school has strict rules, and I am facing suspension or possible expulsion when everything gets done.

If I can't play football, I don't think I could live with myself. I live and breathe football. I don't mind the suspension, but the possibility of expulsion is unthinkable for me. Not being able to play means no college scholarships, and no scholarships means no getting out of this place. Not getting out of this place means not helping my mother and my little sister. And then I might go to jail. I know, I should have known better. I don't want my mom to know, and I sure am not going to tell my sister. I will take care of it my own way.

I can't sleep at night. I can't eat, I am having a very hard time focusing on anything. My grades are suffering, and I can't handle the stress. It's a bit too much for me. So, I have been contemplating what to do. Should I run away? That would mean skipping bail and breaking my curfew. My court date is looming ahead of me. I have no one to talk to. I know I am not crazy, but sometimes I feel like I am carrying the weight of the world on my shoulders. Like I should just quit life, end it all. I was just trying to help. It wasn't supposed to be like this, to end like this. I am still a child, a teenager, but I am facing charges as an adult.

Last week, I finally mustered up enough courage to ask a couple of my friends where to buy a gun, and I got one. I don't know yet what I will do with it. I don't plan on using it…soon. But I feel a need to end it. Some days I have thoughts of going into school with my gun and getting even with my coach, taking it out on the kids who got me in this situation, but the majority of time I just want to go to a lonely place by myself. I blame myself and the universe. I blame my dad and my late uncle. I blame life. I know my anger towards anyone other than myself is misplaced. I hate that I have disappointed myself and my mother, and especially my little sister. In the end, I have myself to blame, that is the truth. I can't live with this type of uncertainty about my future, I don't want to go to jail. I can only think of one way to stop it.

My Dear Sweet Boy,

First, I would like to applaud you for stepping up and being the man of the house when the need arose. That is an excellent quality that I am sure your mom is very proud of. How is she doing by the way? Is she getting any better? How is her depression going?

Have you ever heard of the phrase *"to err is human?"* It is the only phrase that came to mind as I was reading your letter. Evidently life has not been too kind to you. You have made what you thought was the best kind of lemonade with the type of the lemons you have been given. As much as I understand the reasons behind your decision to earn a quick living to help, I wouldn't have advised you to go about it the way you did, and I am sure you now understand why. In a country that is systematically discriminatory to Black and Brown people, especially men, where there is a scarcity of resources available to educate and rehabilitate them, this is the worst decision that you could have made.

The good news is you have a smart head on your shoulders, and you are resourceful. You will overcome this and grow up to accomplish great things. The current happenings are only stumbling blocks in your path. What you don't need to be doing is getting into more trouble and allowing despair to overcome and overwhelm you. Wake up each day and be thankful for it. Remember your sister is looking up to you. Remember your mother is depending on you. Imagine how devastated they would be if anything were to happen to you. I know you love football, and for now, you can probably not see your life or your future without it, but I promise you, it will get better. Many successful people say they grow from their pain. Let this pain be your growing point. Let's be positive about the future. Let's be thankful that you are only suspended and not expelled for now. Something tells me, when push comes to shove, your school will still support you and maybe even put in a good word for you. Can we at least explore that avenue?

Could you reach out to any of your friends' parents? You mentioned how proud of you they all are. That could be a step in the right direction.

~We need to cut ties with the neighborhood kids with the negative influence.

~We need to get you new friends to hang out with.

~We need to get you in with your school counselor to explore your options.

~We need to get you out of the self-blame mindset and into the self-compassion space.

~We need to get you out of the vengeance mindset.

~We need to get rid of the gun right away before someone gets hurt.

May I check back in with you in one month or so? That would really make me feel better.

Yours in the fight,
Dr. Lulu.

Discussion

Did you know that one in five children born in the USA will never grow up with or live with their fathers? I had no idea the number was that high. Whether you call it the "Absent Black Father Syndrome" (ABFS) or "Missing Black Father Syndrome," the point still remains that the absence of the father from the home has been blamed for a great majority of the behaviors and outcomes observed in young African Americans, especially boys. No doubt our teen Damiko, is living a life that in some way is tainted by the absence of his father. He blames his father's absence for some of the events, decisions and outcomes in his life. But, is this completely true? Considering that a father's presence does not mean a father's involvement. How much of his circumstances can we blame on his father's absence?

Is the absence of the father from the home solely responsible for negative outcomes in Black children, or any children for that matter? Does this mean that children raised in homes by mom's (or extended family) do not thrive? Are there no negative outcomes in children from homes with both parents? Have we looked at other issues that might be responsible, or are we all just perpetuating a hype? I too used to have that mindset of singularly blaming the absence of fathers in the home, until I walked the walk of single motherhood and learned the hard way.

Both our 43rd and 44th presidents, George W. Bush and Barack Obama respectively, also bought into the idea and spoke about it many times. President Obama wrote about it, and even launched a program called *"my brother's keeper"* in an attempt to curb the epidemic. The initiative works to expand opportunities for boys and young men of color in underserved communities with a focus on education, reading, job training and mentoring.

Black nuclear families in the United States have been torn apart since the days of slavery, and that is a fact. Luckily, other extended family members have been able to hold up the raising of Black children. However, even after *"slavery has ended,"* factors like the American justice system continues to remove more and more

Black men from the home, and when these men return (if they do), the systems in place essentially strip them of their rights. Those that are not incarcerated face daily threats from police profiling, police brutality and other microaggressions, making it very difficult to be physically and emotionally present in the home.

Institutional racism refers to a system that makes choices that intentionally single out or harm people of a particular race. Structural racism also seeks to accomplish the same goals by creating both legal and tacit systems of racial oppression. These are at the core of the fate of the African American today. Even though studies have shown that children who grow up in two parent homes do better in school and are less likely to end up in a life of crime, these studies have not focused on unequal wages, systemic discrimination, inequality in hiring practices that result in chronic unemployment, housing segregation, and so forth which directly give rise to inequality of educational opportunities, mass incarceration, and ultimately the destruction of the family structure.

Yes, the statistics show that children who grow up without a father are five times more likely to live in poverty and commit crime: nine times more likely to drop out of schools and 20 times more likely to end up in prison, have behavioral problems, or run away from home. Again, no one is focusing on the effect of chronic institutional trauma on these children. Damiko and his sister were exposed to significant trauma early in their short lives. According to the ACEs (discussed in part one), they each have a score of at least 5: parental divorce or separation (feeling of abandonment), emotional insult, family history of incarceration, a family history of suicide and a family history of mental illness (see appendix). That puts them in line for trauma-related disorders including suicidal ideation and early death. Unfortunately, Damiko's current predicament does not help that situation.

A quick google search will show that East and South/Southern Africa also have an epidemic of ABFS with grave side effects and outcomes in their children (see list below). I had no idea about that. Studies from this part of the world focus on its effects on their daughters which is great because most studies tend to focus on the effects on sons. Check out this study done on the women from that part of the world.

In his defense, Damiko did grow up with a father figure in his uncle. He was doing quite well until things started going south with him. This is to say that although absent fathers take the blame for most things, some children do transcend that, and do well despite the circumstances. In the end, life might have thrown him one-too-many balls to juggle.

Effects of Absent Father in the Home According to an article by the Children's Bureau

- A lack of emotional and physical security, and a diminished sense of self.

- Behavioral problems in school (issues with social adjustment, a tendency to hide their emotional issues underneath a cloak of bravado).

- Truancy and poor academic performance, up to 71% of high school dropouts are from a fatherless home. They tend to struggle with academics, critical thinking, math, and truancy. They are less likely to attain academic and professional qualifications in adulthood.

- Delinquency and youth crime, including violent crime. 85 percent of youth in prison have an absent father. Fatherless children are more likely to offend and go to jail as adults. In the US, going to jail as adults underscores a justice system that is strewn with inequality and racial biases.

- Promiscuity and teen pregnancy: fatherless children are more likely to experience problems with sexual health including a greater likelihood of having intercourse before the age of 16, foregoing contraception during first intercourse, becoming teenage parents, and contracting sexually transmitted infection. Girls manifest an object hunger for males, and in experiencing the emotional loss of their fathers egocentrically as a rejection of them, become susceptible to exploitation by adult men.

- Drug and alcohol abuse: fatherless children are more likely to smoke, drink alcohol, and abuse drugs in childhood and adulthood.

- Homelessness. 90 percent of runaway children have an absent father.

- Exploitation and abuse. Fatherless children are at greater risk of suffering physical, emotional, and sexual abuse, they are five times more likely to have experienced physical abuse.

- Abuse and emotional maltreatment. With a *one hundred times* higher risk of fatal abuse, a recent study reported that preschoolers not living with both of their biological parents are 40 times more likely to be sexually abused.

- Physical health problems. Fatherless children report significantly more psychosomatic health symptoms and illness such as acute and chronic pain, asthma, headaches, and stomach aches.

- Mental health disorders. Father-absent children are consistently overrepresented on a wide range of mental health problems, particularly anxiety, depression and suicide.

- Life chances. As adults, fatherless children are more likely to experience unemployment, have low incomes, remain on social assistance, and experience homelessness.

- Future relationships. Father-absent children tend to enter partnerships earlier, are more likely to divorce or dissolve their cohabiting unions and are more likely to have children outside marriage or outside any partnership.
- Mortality. Fatherless children are more likely to die as children and live an average of four years less over their lifespan.

Wow! I had no idea about all these consequences! As a once upon a time single mother, I was shocked when I read some of them. All I could do was check them off one by one as I thought about my sons, thankful that they are growing up well rounded. I would say though, that seeing the statistical results of the effects of ABFS, I am reluctantly changing my mind about my position and I am willing to accept that these studies probably have some truth, but, we must take them with an ounce of salt considering the factors that exacerbate the situation as listed above.

Chapter 19

PARENTAL CONTROL AND EATING DISORDERS

"Beauty is about being comfortable in your own skin. It is about knowing and accepting who you are"

~ Ellen

Sophia

Hi doctor Lulu,

My name is Sophia, but everyone calls me Sophie. I am the first of three daughters born to Chinese parents. I was born in Japan and started elementary school there. My parents lived in Japan because my grandparents lived in Japan. When I was very young, my grandfather passed away, so my grandmother (a retired seamstress) came to live with us, and we moved to live in Beijing. I love my grandmother, but she is tough. My dad traveled a lot for his business, so he wasn't home much. My mom worked part time at a factory, and my grandma was home all the time.

Growing up in a traditional Chinese home, I slowly but surely was made to realize that I did not fit the norm in any way, especially with my weight. You may not know this, but the average Chinese girl is expected to be *"slim, beautiful, successful"* and be a source of pride to her family. Those (dreadful) words have never described me. I have never seen myself as slim, beautiful, or successful. I have always been what you would call *"plump,"* not particularly slim, but not particularly obese. As young Asian girls, a strong sense of belonging is embedded in our upbringing. We are taught early in life, that we should never, on no account bring any form of shame to our families. Little did I know that being overweight was a source of shame to my family! Something as innocent as an extra ounce of fat could earn you an automatic listing in the *"family failure"* category.

As the older of three children, most of the responsibility of *"proper exampling"* laid on my shoulders. I had to do nearly everything right as a child. I had to wake up early enough, do my chores on time, get ready for school on time, perform well in school, and show my little sisters how a *"perfect daughter"* must behave. My parents were hard working, and constantly stressed the need to excel in school, and make straight A's in order to succeed in the future. My grandmother was pushy and direct. I learned early enough from her that I must *"not allow"* myself to get fat or I would not find a good man to marry. She insisted I learn to cook traditional Chinese dishes and eat the right portions to stay slim and attractive and bring pride to our family.

I did my very best to excel in school and though my grades were good, they never seemed to be good enough. I made mostly As, but they were not A+. The harder I tried to be the best student, the harder they pushed for excellence. I found that in those times when things were a bit difficult at home, eating a snack would help my moods. I would sometimes ask for seconds or just go back and take some more food after a meal. Most times my mom would allow it, but my grandma never liked that. My dad always brought snacks and yummies home from his travels, which I enjoyed a lot. Before my teen years my body was still infantile, but things really took a bad turn when I became a teenager, and it began to show on my waistline. I started to plump up a bit, and my grandmother was the very first to notice.

Coincidentally, my family moved to the United States when I turned 13. My dad got a promotion and a transfer to California. My grandmother declined coming with us saying she was not sure she would be able to tolerate the western culture. Truth be told, I was somewhat relieved, and ready to live my life as a free teen! Little did I know things were about to go from a little bad, to a lot worse. You see, back in China, people, especially family members can talk about your weight freely, almost as a term of endearment, to show how much they *"care about you."* It is fair game to discuss your weight at family gatherings, as greetings or salutations, and even as a side comment from a complete stranger on the street! In America, for the most part, discussions about weight are not the norm, at least not in the open, ***except in middle school***!

I arrived in the US bright-eyed, bushy-tailed and ready to conquer the world, but the middle school kids would not have it. They were mean and condescending about everything, from my eyes, to my size, my thick Asian accent, to my haircut and the unique yellowish tinge of my skin. They called me names and made fun of me, since my spoken English was essentially non-existent, they picked on that too. I, on the other hand finally made a pact with food, the more they teased me, the more I ate. The more I ate, the more my mother began to complain. Even though I was trying my very best in school, my grades were simply not good enough, so my dad also began to complain. The more he complained, the more I ate.

Things spiraled out of control when my grandmother came over to visit us that first summer on my mother's insistence, to see if she would like to live in America. She complained and ranted about my size as soon as she saw me at the airport. It did not help matters that she had made me some dresses 3 sizes too small, since she had decided to use my aunt's size to make them. Never mind that my aunt has always had a petite frame and I had big bigger than her even when still lived in Japan! My grandma felt insulted that I couldn't model the dresses. My mother joined in the criticism, she announced that when she was my age, she weighed at least 20lbs less than I was. My grandmother re-told me stories of when they had hardly any food to eat as children and how she and her siblings had to share one small bowl of rice to eat each day.

How she sometimes had only a few grains as her portion, and sometimes went completely without food.

As I got older, things did not improve. My mom once told me that the boys stayed away because I was so *"fat."* At 15yr I had never had a boyfriend. I hated my eyes, my hair, the color of my skin, and the shape of my head. I hated everything about me. I begged my mom to bleach my hair and I secretly nursed a dream to have my eyelids done when I grew up and could afford it. My romance with food continued throughout high school, as much as I hated my body and my weight, I couldn't stop my appetite. One day, while looking through a magazine, I felt very bad inside, seeing the images of skinny models. I felt terrible. I could not stop looking at their slim figures, blonde hair, blue eyes, awesome lips and eyelids. I *wanted* to be like them, I *needed* to be like them. At this time, I had a few friends, and we hung out occasionally, but I was mostly a loner. All my friends were Caucasian, skinny and with blonde hair and blue eyes. I secretly wished I would one day be like them.

I became preoccupied with losing weight, and started looking up ways to get it done, fast. I realized I could skip meals and drink plenty of water to stay hydrated and achieve rapid weight loss. One night, I skipped my dinner, feigning a headache and stomachache. I muttered something about possible food poisoning from the school when my ever-prying grandmother asked. The next morning, I was *really* hungry for breakfast, but I felt victorious! I had skipped one meal, and it hadn't been too bad! By lunch time,

I had a bad headache, but I pushed myself and managed to eat only half of the food on my plate. Another victory! Within a week I had successfully skipped up to 9 meals and was doing fine. I weighed myself for the very first time in my life, 168lbs. At my 5ft 1inch frame, that was considered *"morbidly obese"* and my BMI was off the scales.

Whoa!

Inspired by my success that first week, I slowly became obsessed with my weight, and started to count calories. The problem was getting past my grandmother if I continued to skip my meals. Then I discovered that I could eat as much as I wanted and throw it up soon after, this way, my grandmother would not feel insulted if I didn't eat or empty my plate, and my mother would not fret because I didn't come down to dinner. As much as I hated throwing up, this was a great option. However, I preferred not eating at all, because my weight dropped faster that way. After two more weeks, I was down to 158lbs and life was good. I slowly started checking myself out whenever I passed a mirror or glass windows. By the end of my first month, I could not wait to weigh myself, I was down to 139lbs! I started noticing the stares and the quizzical looks from other students. My grandmother could not hide her joy. She would say stuff like *"you will now be able to attract good boys," "your future is more secure," "you will get a good job"* etc. As much as I dislike listening to my grandmother, I secretly enjoyed this new line of commentary.

At the end of my first three months, I was down to 105 lbs. At this point, my mother started to ask me if everything was ok. I knew it wasn't. But I cheerily said I was fine. In truth, I was tired a lot, my hair was beginning to fall off, my skin had lost its sheen, and my heart would skip beats often. But I was thin, my clothes were loose-fitting, and I was finally the size that my grandmother wanted, right? I had proven that I could be slim. I had proven to myself that I could control at least one part of my life. As much as I enjoyed being in control, *I realize now that I have lost control to an eating disorder.* Sometimes, I can barely focus in school, my grades are beginning to slip, and I now can't stop.

I can't seem to stop myself. I still look fat in the mirror, and I am constantly thinking about food. My science teacher mentioned a need to see a counselor when I confided in her. She encouraged me to tell my parents, and when I did tell my mom and grandmother about my feelings, they both got really upset. *"We are not supposed to tell such to people." "It is not right,"* my grandmother said. She doesn't trust *"those Americans"* as she calls them.

It has been exactly 12 months since I first skipped dinner that night, my weight this morning was 89 lbs. I barely eat anything these days. I am weak, tired and can barely walk most times. Yet, the sight of food not only disgusts, it also scares me. I can't put any food in my mouth, I am afraid I might gain weight. I want to be skinny. I want to make my parents happy. I want to get married and be successful. I want to be worthy of my Chinese ancestry. Yet, I am sad most days, and cry in my bed while trying to fall

116

asleep every night but sleep hardly comes. The teasing in school has mostly stopped though, since I technically got skinny, but it has been replaced with stares and whispers and knowing nods, cat calls and weird looks as I walk by. I hate that I feel sick most times. My parents have continued to look the other way. I don't want to live like this any longer. I don't want to wake up in the mornings anymore. I have no one to turn to at this point.

Could you help me, Dr. Lulu? Please?

Sophie.

Darling Sophie,

Thank you so very much for sharing your story. And thank you so much for reaching out. It is so encouraging to know when one needs help, and to act appropriately. I know it must have been very difficult to do so. You have such a rich Asian heritage and I am proud of you for embracing your roots in all its ramifications, good and bad. It seems though like some of the customs have been more of a burden than a blessing. There is no doubt you have been through a lot, and I completely understand how overwhelming it can be to have all the adults in your family breathing down your neck, seeking to control you from a very young age. These are the same people that were supposed to be there for you. To help you. To guard and guide you. It truly sucks when your parents don't seem to *"really see you."*

Many people don't know that the underlying problem with an eating disorder is not the food. It is often deeper, and more involved. It has to do with control, a fight for control of one's life and emotions. As a woman, I understand that issues concerning our weight are often complex and met with a great deal of sensitivity. For teenage girls, there is so much to unpack: hormones causing physical changes to your body, cliques and ostracization by your peers, dating and its complexities, schoolwork, and exercise. Plus, the need to remain thin which is glamorized on TV and the internet, is mostly pushed to the forefront by Hollywood, social media and so forth.

I understand how difficult and confusing it can be, trying to navigate your way in a world where the homecoming queen is often thin and beautiful, and balancing that with what it means to be beautiful as an Asian teen. I myself have struggled with trying to find my true self, what the word beautiful means to me in reference to my African heritage, and what it means to me in reference to my womanhood. I am only now beginning to understand my unique kind of beauty and realizing that no one out there has any right to define what that should mean to me. Believe me, it is very hard and is a daily struggle for most of us.

My first and most important advice to you is that you must seek medical attention as soon as possible. If you are still having a hard time explaining to your parents, then you could get the help of your science teacher, or your school counselor. They might be able to explain the necessity of immediate treatment to your parents better than you can. Eating disorder treatment depends on which disorder you are diagnosed with. It will include a combination of psychological therapy (psychotherapy), nutrition education, monitoring of your vital signs and internal organs, and sometimes medications.

The treatment will also involve addressing other health problems that might have been caused by your eating disorder which can be serious or even life-threatening if they go untreated for too long. You might need hospitalization or admission into a facility that specializes in eating disorders if you don't improve with standard treatment. Your treatment team will provide an organized approach to your treatment that will help you manage your symptoms and return you to a healthy weight in order to regain your physical and mental health again. So, the good news is it is treatable, but one must start early, and it might not be easy.

The road to recovery can be long and difficult. It is often laden with pain and stress. You must learn to trust again, be it your family members, your providers or even yourself. You have to be willing to allow yourself to get better. To give up control just a little bit. I have had a few patients who have had eating disorders, I must say that each one was strong-willed, and it was tough treating them, but they all eventually got better. I hope and wish the same for you. You do have a bright future and your whole life ahead of you.

Again, thank you for being brave enough to reach out and ask for help. Thank you for reaching out specifically to me. I truly appreciate your trust and will be right here holding your hand as you navigate your way back to health. The bottom line is to focus on self-love and self-compassion and try to let go of the need to be in control. The road back to health will not be easy, but it is certainly the best road forward.

Yours in self-love,

Dr. Lulu.

Discussion

Asians have very strong family cohesiveness, with roots that are deeply embedded in Confucian theories. This cohesive trait though sometimes envied by other ethnicities, can become a source of serious issues in some families. The extreme need to be successful and almost perfect has driven many-an-Asian kid into self-destructive behaviors. Unfortunately, eating disorders are now becoming more prevalent as a result of that situation. Records show that Asian American college women express more body dissatisfaction than their Caucasian counterparts.

According to a viral article that was published in 2003, the shame-based-culture is a trait unique to Asian families. Their life's choices can end up affecting the reputation of their family. This sometimes-unrealistic expectation can be a source of extreme stress especially in their teenagers who are already dealing with a lot of stress from adolescence. In their culture, successes of offspring are equated with success of the family and is often associated with an elevated status in the family. Some families can go as far as castigating their children who disgrace the family name. This tendency is also exacerbated by those of us who view people of Asian ancestry as a *"model minority,"* a sociological term which has stuck because of their ability to survive in America through academic excellence, tireless work ethic and strong family bonds, I guess my question is at what price?

Being fat in an Asian family is understood to be an indication of personal weakness, lack of discipline, laziness, or failure. The Asian culture magnifies this by allowing their citizens to be brutally honest when making comments about physical appearances. It is not unusual to be called *"fat"* by family members, acquaintances or even strangers on the streets. Giving rise to the *"thin but not necessarily healthy"* theme. Contradictorily, when at family gatherings or even at home, you are not only expected to eat and finish everything on your plate, you are also expected to eat extras if offered to avoid being *"rude."* Unfortunately, with their singular definition of beauty as *"petite, pale and thin,"* Asians, especially women, get caught up in the nightmare of uncertainty not only where their weight is concerned, but also worry about other aspects of their body like their eyes and hair. When coupled with the need to also excel in school and only make honor roll-worthy grades one can see how emotional issues like body dissatisfaction can easily ensue.

The face of eating disorder is slowly changing from a cis-gendered, straight, White female to Asian, Black or Hispanic youth. Studies show that youth from all these ethnicities have reported attempting to lose weight at similar rates. Due largely to stigma attached to mental illness and seeing a psychologist, many youths especially those of Asian ancestry do not seek medical help and mostly suffer in silence. Partially from ignorance, Asian parents often respond to requests for mental health with dismissiveness, frustration, fear, denial, anger and even blame, often asking their ward why they are doing that to themselves. This kind of reaction can further be a hindrance to early diagnosis and management of the disorder, leading to potential life-threatening complications, including suicide.

Compounding the situation more, is the acute shortage of providers and specialists in the healthcare community with diverse ethnic backgrounds to provide care across all cultural spectrums. There is a need to create awareness and provide culture-appropriate clinical training for providers. There is also a dire need for the cycle to break, and that responsibility would fall on parents to become aware of the effects of exerting excessive control and demanding unrealistic expectations of their children.

Chapter 20

CHILD MARRIAGE AND SUICIDE

"We have a vision where women and girls live in dignity, are healthy, have choices and equal opportunities"

~ Foundation for Women's Health,

Research and Development

Anisha

Hello Dr. Lulu,

I want to thank you immensely for this opportunity to share my story with you. I am unsure if there is much that can be done at this time about my situation, by the time you receive this letter... After reading my story, I hope you will understand a bit more about my plight, and not arrive at any unfair conclusions. I know some might understand, many might not, but at this point it really doesn't matter anymore.

A couple of years ago, I had pretty much resigned to my fate, as designed by my parents. But in recent times, I am thinking there is no need to resign to a life of certain unhappiness. I shouldn't have to live my life like a second- or third-class citizen in my homeland. I will no longer accept my *"fate."* This is not the life for me. I shall NOT be marrying anybody, and that is a fact!

My story will begin when I was 3yrs old and still living in my hometown of Jharkhand, in the Eastern part of India. A relatively rural state rich in natural resources but plagued by poverty. My hometown has often been described as having a *"paradox of plenty,"* or a *"resource curse."* Meaning it is a nation blessed with natural resources, but lacking in economic growth, development and democracy. Though Jharkhand is famous for some of its landmarks like the *Hindu Sun Temple,* a majority of us live below the India poverty line, with widespread malnutrition in children. The main language spoken is Hindi, and the main religion practiced here is Hinduism, followed by Islam. Both religions unfortunately support childhood marriage, and my state has one of the highest rates of child-hood marriage in India.

Childhood marriage is why my story begins when I turned 3, the age of my betrothal. My husband-to-be was a 6yr old son of a gold mine worker colleague of my father. We are both from the same caste system. I am the only child of my parents who are staunch Hindus, and we are very poor. My mother is a homemaker. My maternal grandmother, a *"perpetual widow,"* lived with us for a portion of my childhood until she died a few weeks before my 9th birthday. I never knew my maternal grandfather, he died when my mother was only 2yrs old, and according to the Hindu tradition, my grandma was not allowed to remarry. This idea baffled me a lot.

I loved my grandmother a lot. The one thing I will always remember is the smell of her jasmine scented hair. A fragrance that I catch a whiff of occasionally even to this day (when her spirit comes around to check on me). She was a beautiful woman, but widowhood affected her psychologically. When I was much younger, I would sit on the kitchen floor next to her, watching her delicate hands as she prepared dinner. My favorite was the curry and rice, the sweet smells filled up the entire expanse of our tiny home.

I learned a lot from her. When I asked about the perpetual widow process, she explained that being a Hindu widow was essentially a *"social death."* Many of them are ostracized even by their own children! Most of them were married off at very young ages to much older men who often die not long after the marriage, leaving these poor women to a life of poverty in deplorable conditions, facing disease, loneliness and mental anguish for the rest of their natural lives. In essence, widows are not allowed to remarry in certain areas that still adhere to the archaic traditions. Ironically widowers can, and often do remarry.

I watched my grandmother suffer in silence, sentenced to a life of dependency on her son-in-law for her upkeep. But she was one of the lucky ones, most of them are completely shunned by their family members. She told me stories of women, widows who paid the ultimate price by sacrificing their lives following the deaths of their husbands. A process called *"sati"* or self-immolation (throwing one's self into the cremation fire of their husband). When I asked her what she thought about *sati*, she said she had actually considered it, but couldn't go through with it because my mom was still so young when my grandfather died.

My grandmother taught me to be strong and resilient, she stressed the need to be independent and never give up on my hopes and dreams. She also stressed the need for education and taught me to dream. And dream I did. I loved school, and dreamed of one day growing up, going to college and becoming a lawyer. She told me India needs me, the women and children of India especially need me. *"We need a strong female voice to fight for us, to fight all the societal ills, all the social injustice, the inequality, the harsh laws that disenfranchise women"* she said. She told me she had picked my name, Anisha. It is short for, *"Anishchitata"* meaning *"a goddess of darkness"*. *"A"* means without and *"Nisha"* means night which basically means nightless or sleepless, because according to her, I had been chosen to do the work that needed to be done in India, tirelessly and without rest.

So back to my betrothment. I remember the day my parents told me about it like it was yesterday. I had just turned 12yrs old. My father returned from work, very excited, which was not like him. He is usually sulky, frowning and complaining about the hard work with little pay at the mines. He called me into our tiny living room where I found my mom sitting on the even tinier dining table, head bowed. She looked like she had been crying. I couldn't imagine what could have happened. I had a bit of *deja vu* with a flash back to the day my grandmother passed, this was a familiar scene, except this time, my dad was happy, and my mom was sad. Last time, they were both sad.

My mother, like my grandmother had wanted me to get an education, to escape a future of poverty and unhappiness. Initially I could not understand why they were both so adamant that I finish school. One day, while fixing my hair up for a wedding, my mom eventually told me that my grandmother had gotten betrothed at age 6 and married at 11. She herself, had been betrothed at age 9 and married at age 13 to my father. As their only child, I never thought I would ever face that kind of future. I simply didn't. I guess I was naive and silly to think that somehow my father would skip tradition, defy the odds and allow me to grow up free.

My father started by reminding me that I am Hindu, and that marriage is a sacred and necessary path to my future as a woman. As soon as the word *marriage* came out of his mouth, I didn't hear anything else. My heart stopped and my world seemed to stop along with it. I immediately felt my stomach lurch and somehow its contents found their way through my mouth. My head hurt and my knees felt like jelly, and rather rapidly, the floor found my face. I vaguely remember being picked up by my mom's shaky arms and carried to my bed.

"You were betrothed when you were 3 years old," my mother said to me when I came to. *"What?"* *"How come I didn't know about it?"* *"We didn't feel a need to tell you too soon,"* she

127

responded. *"I am so sorry, I wish things were different,"* she added sadly. *"This would have never happened if grandma was still alive!"* I yelled. *"Your grandmother knew about it,"* she said in a soft almost inaudible voice. *"So, I am going to be married to a boy that I have never met?"* *"How could you have allowed this, mama?"* Sadly, I knew the answers to all my questions, but asked them anyway. I have lived in this house and watched my mother being treated like a second-class citizen by my father and his brothers. She is largely silent, married to bear children, but she only bore one. She has never spoken a harsh word. In India, women are essentially raised to have no voice, to never speak up, or be recognized. She was never argumentative, and hardly ever got in conflict with my father. He has the first and last say all the time, and I hate him for that.

As I said earlier, I hadn't believed that as an only child, this could be possible. I have however known most of my life that this was a probability. It happens more than you would like to know. There are towns and villages where up to 80% of children are betrothed and married off by the age of 6yrs. I just hoped and somehow believed that it would not happen to me. A part of me died that day. The part that loved to dream. The part that wanted to live, the part that was to go to law school and help save the women and girls (and boys) of my village. The worst part is, ***I have to drop out of school to become a wife.*** I have to move in with my future husband's family to begin my role as a wife at the age of 14! The wedding is planned for next year, next May to be exact, to coincide with *Akshaya Tritiya*, a Hindu holiday. And I have never even met my future husband.

I have become very sad and depressed. I still can't believe it. My life as I know it is over. I shall become another person's property, a mere boy himself. And if he somehow dies at this age, I will have to live a life of solitude and shame as a perpetual widow like my beloved grandmother who became a widow at the age of 16!

A few months have passed since my parents broke the news to me, and they have slowly started preparations for the wedding. As I write this, I am extremely sad and believe I have gone into full blown depression. I hardly speak to anyone at home. I stay by myself a lot these days, thinking, planning, deciding what my next move will be. I know deep inside that I will not marry him. That's the one thing I know for sure. My options are to either flee the house and become a runaway, risking certain life on the streets and slums, or I could end my life.

There is a local train that runs three times a week to and from the mines, only a few kilometers from our home. I will study its schedule well and know exactly when I can go there. I remember another girl from a neighboring village who had taken some poison and ended her life because she was betrothed, another ran away and I heard she joined a notorious prostitution ring. In the last 2 weeks, two girls have died by throwing themselves in front of the train, and many more are thrown into despair and depression for childhood dreams cut short.

I don't really know what to do now. My days are long and dreary, I can't get through to my father about this. It's way too late.... The dowry has already been paid. My mother, herself a child bride knows deep down how I feel. She knows the feeling of hopelessness and helplessness that overcomes someone who has no say in her life, or her future. I have never met this boy that I am supposed to be marrying. I am no longer able to go to school, all my dreams are shattered, I hate myself and my life. I don't want to live this way. I will *not* become a slave to anyone, to a religion, or to an archaic tradition that robs little girls and boys of their futures. I will not give up all my dreams...

As I sit here with my thoughts, writing this letter to you, my mom silently walks into my bedroom. She has something colorful in her hands. They are two scarves. She does not say a word, she simply places one of the scarves next to my hand on the bed and walks out of the room. I pick it up and follow her... She does not stop walking until she gets to the dark hallway that leads to the back of the house... My father is not home yet. My eyes get used to the darkness with the help of cracks in the ceiling. I can make out the silhouette of two looped ropes suspended on the huge wooden beam used to build our roof, with two chairs placed directly beneath each one. She walks up to the first chair, climbs on it, grabs the first rope, and ties her scarf around her eye as a blindfold. I instinctively follow suit. I whisper *"thank you"* to her, hug her legs and hold on for a little longer before climbing onto the other chair. Just before I tie my blindfold, I smell it, it is ever so strong, Jasmine! My grandmother! I smile and offer a quick heavenward thanks because I know exactly what I must do next. I grab the second rope and loop it over my neck as I hear my mother push off her chair, a second later, I do the same.

Discussion

According to UNICEF, on a global scale, every 3 seconds a young girl under the age of 18 is married off. This amounts to 25,000 girls every day! And if this trend continues, 100 million girls will be married off in the next decade. Let that sink in for a minute.

The Prohibition of Child Marriage Act of 2006 is basically ignored in India, as scores of young girls as young as 6 to 8 years old are subjected to marriage, often to men old enough to be their fathers. Arranged, and early marriages, young motherhood, low socioeconomic status, total disregard of the female of the species, and domestic violence are factors that contribute to the high female suicide rate. India, a highly patriarchal country lacks any protective element for women. Though illegal, child marriage still exists in India, and it has the highest number of child brides in the world. While child marriage is overall on the decline in India, countless girls like Anisha from poor regions continue to slip through the cracks. More than a quarter of Indian girls are married before the legal age of 18 years, and nearly as many boys before their legal age of 21 years. Largely thought to occur as a result of poverty and illiteracy in rural India, there have also been reports of child marriages in the metropolitan areas of India as well.

Even in these modern days, the average Indian woman is most times regarded as inferior to the man. She is often married off as a child and remains a perpetual widow in the case of an early death of her husband even if she is still an infant! In certain parts of Rural India, mass marriages still occur. A great majority of these brides and grooms are all under-age and most of them were betrothed as early as their toddler years. Despite a plunge in the rate of child marriages over the past decade, there are still more underage brides in India than any other country in the world. Some families reportedly consider their daughters a liability, an economic burden, and would rather marry them off than having to deal with feeding and caring for them, thus transferring the responsibility to their husbands. Most of the girls drop out of school as soon as their marriage ceremony is done, some do it earlier in order to save money for payment of the dowry, which the bride's parent is responsible for.

Sadly, I must add that in Nigeria where I was born and went to medical school, this exact scenario also plays out. It occurs widely across the country in nearly all the tribes. In our case, these girl-brides can also often be the second, third or fourth wives. Most of them become mothers as mere children themselves. They face a great degree of poverty and harsh socio-economic conditions, and the cycle continues.

In northern Nigeria where I went to medical school, many of these young mothers develop vesico-vaginal fistulas or VVF: an abnormal opening and connection between the urinary bladder and the wall of the vagina or anus, resulting in urine or stool leakage through the vagina. This is often a complication of extremely prolonged labor and damage to the affected tissues when the head of a baby is trapped in a small pelvis of a child-mother. The prolonged labor occurs as a result of poverty, decreased availability and access to medical care during labor, disproportionately large head of the baby compared to the young mothers' contracted pelvises, and lack of follow up care immediately postpartum. At last check, there are nearly 1 million Nigerian women living with this disease. Not only do these young women suffer from VVF, they also face a high maternal and infant mortality rate, domestic abuse (physical and emotional), social isolation, divorce, and mental health issues like depression which all further compound their situation.

It is easy then to see why suicide is a quick choice and outlet for many of these women. Seeking treatment for mental illness or stress is often met with stigma, shame, fear and major roadblocks with access to care. It is not uncommon to hear about mass suicides, or family suicides in India, however, in a country where an attempted suicide was punishable by a fine and up to a year in prison until recently, it becomes imperative that any suicide attempts must therefore result in suicide deaths.

Chapter 21

INTERNAL CONFLICT

AND

EXTERNAL REJECTION

"My son is gay. I knew that as early as the age of 19months"

~ Dr. Lulu

Emeka

Hi Dr. Lulu,

I am not entirely sure where to begin with my story, but I will take a jab at it. I can start by stating my name, Emeka... I am the first of two sons born to hardworking and dedicated West African parents, my mom, a Ghanaian, met my dad, a Nigerian while they were studying at New York University (NYU). My father was an engineering major, and my mom was a nursing student at that time. Despite all the difficulty with their cultural differences they were both bent on getting married which they did, amid major objections from my grandparents back home, I am told. My dad now works with British Petroleum (BP) gas in Port Harcourt, in the South Eastern part of Nigeria. My mom is a stay at home mom. We live a fairly comfortable life. I can't complain, and neither can my brother, but my mom complains a lot, especially when my dad travels out of town for work, which seems to be all the time these days.

My father and I don't really get along. As far back as I can remember, we never have. He has always thought I am weak, wimpy, soft spoken and therefore not fully worthy of being called his son. My father is a titled chief you see, and in Igboland where we are from, the first son should be seen as strong, masculine, a leader, and a warrior. *"You are too much like your mother,"* he would often say in his thick Igbo accent, when I was in mid childhood, *"you need to toughen up and act like a man." "No son of mine is going to be walking around this house acting like a woman."* I hated those words and still do.

Just a bit of a background: my parents moved back to Nigeria after they each completed their advanced education. I was born a few months afterwards. They had both been Catholics when they met, and I was born and baptized in the Catholic church. However, somewhere along the line my mother saw the light, and switched to what she now calls the *"saved church."* She is pretty much a nurse-turned evangelist and my father hardly attends Mass anymore. It seems the less interested my father is in any church, the deeper my mother goes into her own church. Over the years I have watched them slowly move further and further away from each other emotionally, there is no semblance of love or affection between them. Nigerian (Igbo) men typically do not express emotions that will deem them *"soft and emasculated,"* so no surprises there, but my mom on the other hand... Watching them has strengthened my resolve to wait until I meet that certain someone who will share everything I believe in with me for a perfect happily after. Talking about love and marriage, that is sort of why I am writing this, but...

I live in Nigeria, my given Igbo name is, *"Chukwuemeka,"* meaning *"God has done it all or God has done well."* Since I had a fair share of my upbringing in my father's hometown, I do understand some of the native Igbo tongue and have always mused to myself, about my name. What were my parents thinking when they named me that? Were they hoping for a, *"perfect child"* a *"perfect son?"* Am I that perfect child, that perfect son? If God is indeed infallible and omniscient, why then did He choose to create me this way? Why was I born to traditional West African parents? Why do I have an unyielding, patriarchal Nigerian father and a soft, weak-spirited Ghanaian mother. Why?

As far back as I can remember, I have always felt different. I have felt like a misfit, like the world was revolving around me, but I was rooted in one spot. I tried to live my life to emulate those around me, I tried to blend in as much as I could. I knew deep within me that I had to live as *"normally and as plainly"* as I could. The alternative was not an option. I could never skip a beat. I was

136

after all, the first son of an Igbo chief, whose title must be guarded and respected, knowing that someday, I too will have to earn my own chieftaincy title, even if I hated the idea and my entire being disagreed with it.

I think I first suspected that I was gay at the age of 9. It crossed my mind the day I went to school and while playing at recess, I tripped on something and fell face first onto the dirt. He ran up to me, turned me around and had the most concerned look on his face, because he thought he had pushed me a bit too hard and I fell. He stretched out his right hand for me to grab it and pull myself up. My heart was racing so fast in my chest, I couldn't tell if it was as a result of the fall or as a result of his hold. I remember wanting to spend the rest of the afternoon playing with just him so I could hold his hand more, but he was already back at play with the other boys in our grade. So, I tucked the experience away in my brain's hard drive.

Around age 11 years, I knew for sure. It was at his 11th birthday. As I walked into their well decorated living room, I saw him dressed in his Sunday best holding tightly to his little sister's hand. He was taking her to their mom. He bent down and whispered something in her ear to which she nodded happily. I imagined he was telling her something funny like, *"I will let you play with all my new toys, if you stay with mom until my friends leave, ok?"* After that day I still thought it was a stupid childhood crush that would soon wear off. I went about my business trying my best to blend in and banish any thoughts of liking another male who is not a relative, to a far-away-land.

My mother says she has always known. She says she knew when I was only an infant. She says she knew I was not like other boys, and she had even confided in her own mother and her sister-in-law back then, much to their great chagrin. They were so appalled at even the thought of it, that she was forbidden from ever bringing the topic up again with words like, *"Never!" "The devil is a liar!" "That will never be our portion!"* and *"Tufiakwa!"* (God forbid).

I still remember the day she called me upstairs and took me into one of the large walk-in closets (ironically) in her bedroom to question me, at that time I was 17 and about to graduate from high school. She asked me to sit down, and she sat opposite me. Trying her best not to look directly into my eyes. I could tell she was nervous. My mom is extremely soft spoken, kind-hearted and prayerful. Since my father's infidelity began, she has slowly become even more prayerful and always has a bible verse for every situation. One would think my father was making up for not marrying a Nigerian woman, he was now having Nigerian girlfriends and what I call *"sugar daughters"* outside the marriage. My mom always confided in me. She would tell me again and again, how disappointed she was in my father for his decisions. I thought this was one of those sessions, but it wasn't.

She started with a statement about how a life of sin would surely lead to hell. She recited a couple of bible verses about homosexuality, certain death and hellfire. Then she asked me if I think I am gay, because if I am, the Apostle at church could help me. Her *"prayer warriors"* could lay hands on me and pray for me and pray the evil spirit of homosexuality away. She asked me not to lie to her because she already knew. *"A mother always knows,"* she said. When I asked her how she knew, she *said, "you never wanted to play with toy cars, or any traditional boy-toys for that matter." "You always wanted soft plush animals" "You would sit for hours hugging them as you listened to soft music on the radio." Sometimes you would even cry to the melody." "You have never been a boy's boy," "I will always love you, however, it is sinful, and your soul will surely end in hell if you continue that way."* I tried to rationalize with her. If she had always known since I was a baby, meaning I was born this way, then how is it that I am *"committing a sin?"* She didn't respond, just reminded me that I was going off to university soon, and this was not a good thing to continue with.

I shook my head, begging for the session to end. How completely senseless is that? To know your child was born a certain way and turn around and blame the child for it! And then banish the child to hell fire? Did she even ever want me? Did she not ask her God for me? Were my parents not excited about having their first child like any other new parents? If so, then why this backlash? She was planning to take me for special prayer sessions at the church. She had been promised by the apostle that they could and would pray it out of me, and that nothing is impossible for God. She even hinted that one of the apostles had seen

139

a vision about one of her children who needed prayers, and she knew right away that it was me. I tried to explain that any child going off to the university would certainly need prayers, not necessarily because they are gay, but it fell on deaf ears. She was going to pay the equivalent of $2,000 to him for the special brand of prayers needed. Hmmm, I shook my head in disbelief, not only did the Apostle know she had the means, he also knew she was quite gullible!

I felt trapped. Up until this point, the only person I had ever said anything to about my sexuality was my younger brother. A few years ago, he had come up to me asking for some dating advice. He was 14 and I was 16. I muttered something about not having any advice since I hadn't dated before. *"Well maybe it's because you are gay!"* he retorted. I turned sharply, looked directly into his eyes and asked where he got that idea from. He giggled and said he was just joking. However, because of my abrupt reaction, as he turned around to leave, he stopped in his tracks, spun around really slowly with furrowed brows, a quizzical look on his face and a *"please say it ain't so"* look in his eyes. I shrugged and said, *"I didn't create myself you know."* After a long hard look, he walked up to me patted my back, and nodding slowly, he declared, *"you are my only brother and I will always love you." "I might not understand it, but I know you are the coolest guy and best big brother ever! So, if you are gay, then I know that God, in His perfect wisdom, made you that way."* I got up, hugged him real hard, and spent the rest of the afternoon telling him all about it. And swore him to secrecy... I could tell he was confused and concerned at the same time. He promised not to tell anyone, but wondered loudly why I didn't simply tell someone, and put an end to my misery. His only concern was also my only concern, how our dad would take it.

He has been bugging me to tell someone since then, so I am telling you now, Dr. Lulu. I turn 22 on my next birthday come August, and I am currently at a major crossroads in my life. I shall be graduating from medical school in a few months. That experience itself, was something else, maybe a story for another day. I hope to possibly move to the US or Canada for a pediatric residency when I graduate, but my heart is still heavy-laden, and I am having the hardest time figuring out what to do. To this day I have never allowed myself to date, and never engaged in any form of relationship. I am still a virgin. Not because I haven't had any crushes or romantic interests, but because I am half Nigerian and half Ghanaian. Two of the worst countries to be born gay in today's world. While in college, one time I thought about trying online dating, some friends had done that to meet girls, and they had been successful with it. I thought I could use it to my advantage, only to discover that the Nigerian government has banned homosexuality, and it is punishable by imprisonment. To make things worse, unscrupulous citizens are using the dating apps to trick gay men. They trap them into a meeting, beat them up, rape them and might even kill them. This is the kind of country I live in, so that is a no-go.

My main dilemma is that I want to tell my father about my sexuality. Partly because I know he is expecting me to settle down and get married soon. While it is not mandatory to marry at an early age anymore, I know that as a first son, I will need to show some interest in women, soon. Presently, I don't have any plans for that. When my friends at home ask me about a girlfriend, I always say she is a school relationship, and flip the story when my friends at school ask about *"her."* I find myself increasingly sad. I know my mother is concerned about it as well, she gives me a very weird look sometimes and I just know what she is thinking. My plan is to inform my father when I get home this summer, and while I know he will partly be responsible for financing my further education overseas, I also can't help but wonder what will happen when I tell him. I fear the worst, he might disown me.

You see, he is the typical alpha male. Fearless, focused and fierce. He is a typical *"Africámán"* (Broken English). He always reminds my brother and I that he is a descendant of warriors and survivors. The Biafrans. Such men can only bear strong masculine sons who will go on to bear them more sons. If I do come out to him and the rest of my extended family, I fear that the whole debacle between my mother, my grandmother and aunt long ago, might come back to haunt her. Being the superstitious people that we are, somehow, some bad juju stuff is bound to come out to the surface. My mother is a foreigner in Nigeria, I fear she might be sent back home to Ghana after these many years of marriage. It is the way we do things here. We only want to have perfect children. ***Not broken gay ones.*** You see, in some parts of my country, when a child perceived as *"defective,"* their mother is often to blame, and that could be grounds for a divorce. When things don't go as expected, they either throw the Bible at it, or throw black magic at it, and sometimes, both. Such hypocrisy.

So, in as much as I worry about the interplay between myself, my sexuality and the country I was born in, I worry more about my mother, my younger brother and the consequences of my coming out. What will *"a scandal"* like this do to them? It is a daily and constant struggle for me. I also worry about furthering my education. What will happen? How can I afford to live out my dreams for the future? As for my father, I don't only fear his wrath, I also worry about what the rest of his extended family members will say. What about my mother's Ghanaian family? I have often wondered if there are other family members who are could also be LGBTQ+. I read somewhere that it does runs in the family. Are they therefore leading double lives, living in denial? Could I truly be alone in this?

As the end of school draws near, and graduation is within reach, I have been really conflicted and very stressed out. I have my final exams and this huge decision to come out hanging over my head. I need something to do to help me cope with all the conflicting thoughts. I can't really talk to anyone, neither a friend nor a professional. Counseling is not yet much of an option in Nigeria. Even if there were a good option for counseling, I fear that I might not have the confidentiality that I need for my situation. I also fear a backlash from the counselors who might also be biased against my sexuality or might want to throw their religion and prayers at me.

Last weekend while at a friend's birthday party on campus, the drinks were passing around. Never been a drinker, I turned it down. Then one of my very few friends, Chidi, suggested something else that would *make me feel better right away.* Funny enough he said it was cough medicine. *"Ummm, dude, how will some cough medicine help me feel better?"* I asked him. He said, *"just try it, a trial will convince you."* Ha! I initially hesitated, wondering how da heck and when cough medicine became a recreational drink, but I took one bottle and put it in my back pocket. He was right, I *do* want to feel better. I *do* want my pain to stop. I want to come out to my father. I am tired of living like this. I will try anything to avoid feeling this way. I don't think I really want to end my life, but I also know that in recent times many Nigerian teens and young adults are resorting to rat poison called *SNIPER* to kill themselves. I am not sure how I feel about that. It sounds painful.

When I got to my dorm that evening, I took out the bottle, and looked at the dark liquid inside. It smelt sweet, a strawberry aroma. Its label read, *Panadeine.* It contains 500 mg of Paracetamol and 8 mg of Codeine. I wondered how in the world this was going to make me feel better and *"forget my troubles"* like Chidi suggested. I shrugged. At this point, I have only a little to lose, I recognize Paracetamol as the pain medicine, know that the other ingredient is a narcotic. I have heard about the cough medicine addiction that is sweeping across the country and affecting the youth *en mass.* I

144

am guessing this is it. I don't plan on getting addicted or anything, besides, I only have this single bottle. How much damage can just one bottle do? As for the *SNIPER*, I am contemplating buying one bottle as well, just in case. I know that it has enough poison to kill several people. I know its active ingredient is an organophosphate. I don't think I can kill myself for something that I didn't choose to be, but the thought has definitely crossed my mind. I am only getting the stuff ready in case my situation worsens when I come out to my parents and family members as planned.

Another option I am considering is simply not returning home. I just can't face the negativity and hypocrisy. On the one hand, my parents are Christians and church going people, on the other hand, if indeed I am *"fearfully and wonderfully made"* by God who is infallible, then how come they are quick to judge and ostracize me? Does it mean that God made a mistake when he was creating me? Is this really a good doctrine to believe in and preach? Are there no LGBTQ+ people in the church? Are there no gay priests and pastors on the pulpit? What do you think, Dr. Lulu?

Looking forward to hearing back from you.

Emeka

Dear Emeka,

I can't even begin to tell you just how sorry I am that you are going through this. Indeed, it is a tough situation that you have on your hands. With your parents on opposing sides of the table, and nearly no support on the home front, I can only imagine how hard things must be for you. The good news is you have a supportive sibling, at least you will have someone on your side of the court when you get home. Are you really serious about not returning home? I understand fully how tough it must be to have some hostility at the home base, but not returning home is a bit dangerous. I know you literally feel trapped and even overwhelmed by it all but running away is not a good line of thinking. Do you have any relatives, aunts or uncles you could go to their homes instead? They might be able to speak to your parents about your predicament. I know that is one way to get around to Nigerian parents, but if they don't understand or support your sexuality, that could be an issue too.

I would never advise you to purchase *SNIPER* on any condition. I would also advise you to get rid of the cough medicine that you already have in your possession as soon as possible. As a soon to be medical doctor, you know the dangers of narcotic abuse. Nothing is so bad that it cannot be discussed, and solutions found. I completely understand your story and I hear you, however, harming yourself can never be a good way out.

Do you have a school student adviser? Are there any counselors available for you at school? Any of your friends' parents who you could confide in? We must find a trusted adult. They might even be able to accompany you home to help you break the news to your parents, or at least intercede for you. I don't advise you to do it alone, that might end badly. One good news is that you are now an adult and about to graduate from medical school! Congratulations by the way! The worst-case scenario is you move out of the home, get a job, and start a new life on your own, if your father does carry out the threat that you are so fear he might. You can most certainly get a decent job and save up money for your residency as you take your foreign medical graduate exams. I would prefer that to running away. The streets are very dangerous, and all kinds of bad things could happen to you out there if your exit strategy is not properly planned.

One other thing you could do is get with some of your trusted friends and move in together as you all start your new lives. I know you want to go on to do your right residency way, that might have to wait while you get your living situation taken care of. I have learned that God does answer all prayers, but sometimes His answer is either *"no,"* or *"not yet."*

I would focus on school for now though, as tough as that might be. Finish up with good grades and then we can deal with your parents and family afterwards. I know that at this time, it seems like you can't see past your problems, but, in the grand scheme of things, this is really not that bad. You are alive, you are healthy, you have the rest of your life ahead of you, and I might add, a trusting, fruitful and lasting relationship with your soulmate ☺. It could be much worse.

There are lots of support groups out there for gays and lesbians, many of them accept members virtually. Social media has an endless online support potential. These days, thanks to telemedicine, you can receive counseling online, and on your phone... They can be very effective. I know for a fact that Nigeria has an all-volunteer counseling group called Mentally Aware Nigeria Initiative (MANI) that offer free coaching and counseling sessions anonymously (see info in the resources part of this book).

Again, I thank you for caring enough about yourself to tell me about your problems. I hope I have been able to give you some practical suggestions to try. I will be very open to reconnecting with you later in the year, after your graduation. Oh, and by the way, congratulations again, it is well deserved, now go on and conquer those exams! All the very best!

Yours in activism,

Dr. Lulu.

Discussion

With a population of nearly 200 million (198,929,968 as of February 2019), Nigeria is the most populous country in Africa, with Ethiopia as a distant second, and South Africa coming in third. Nestled in the Western corner of the great continent and surrounded by a combination of French-speaking and English-speaking countries, Nigeria is regarded as one of the more *"progressive"* countries amongst its neighbors. It is however unfortunate that this *"Giant of Africa"* is still heavily plagued by an epidemic of *"third world diseases."* Nearly crippled with widespread corruption from its governing bodies and the societal ills that accompany that (extreme poverty, widespread crime, religious proliferation, tribalism, kidnapping, child marriage, prostitution, and sex trafficking, to name a few), Nigeria is on top of its *"F"* game.

The widespread intolerance, persecution, blackmail and prejudice towards the LGBTQ+ community of Nigeria is the main issue in Emeka's story. His situation is not unique, however. Did you know that in Nigeria, if *"caught,"* members of the LGBTQ community face up to 14 years imprisonment according to a federal law that prohibits all forms of homosexuality? Former president Goodluck Jonathan signed The Same Sex Marriage Prohibition Act in May of 2013. Predictably, Nigeria is not alone, similar laws have been passed by 36 of the 54 African countries, some of these countries actually have a death penalty as punishment for same-sex couples. This discovery prompted the UK Guardian to describe Africa as *"the world's most homophobic continent."* In countries like The Central African Republic and Benin Republic, same-sex relations are not specifically illegal, but their laws heavily discriminate against gays and outrightly treat straight people differently.

Ironically, Africa has its own rich heritage of same-sex relationships dating as far back as time. My own people, the Igbos, have a history of lesbianism that surprised me. There are even reports of female healers who explain their lesbianism by saying that they are possessed by male ancestral spirits, and argue that it was practiced to further patriarchy. According to an article by Nigerian-born, openly gay HIV/LGBTQ+ Activist Bisi Alimi, who wrote, *"So, what*

149

accounts for the current dismissal of homosexuality on the continent? One factor is the increased popularity of fundamental Christianity, by way of American televangelists, since the 1980s. While Africans argued that homosexuality was a western import, they, in turn, used a western religion as the basis for their argument. When I have challenged people who are anti-gay, many have said that it is not our culture. However, when you probe further, they argue that homosexuality is not in the Bible. But the Bible is not our historical culture. This shows there is a real confusion about Africa's past. Reinforcing this is the fact that populist homophobia has kept many politicians in power. Across Africa, if you hate gay people (openly), you get votes."

With this type of past, it would appear that colonialism and western religion have influenced social attitudes to LGBTQ+ people in Africa today. Not entirely surprising therefore, as Mr. Alimi argues, most African countries use religion as their main defense for anti-gay propaganda, much like their colonial western countries, with the United States as a prototype.

It is no wonder our young man, Emeka is at a major crossroad. He is not only dealing with his father's potential reaction to his coming out as gay, he is also facing intolerance and discrimination from his extended family, his community, as well as both countries of his dual citizenship. Therefore, we can understand why he has become depressed and about to succumb to the possible use of illicit substances to drown his sorrows. The worst part is that he also experiences intermittent suicidal ideations. This is not a

150

complete surprise, as many youths who contemplate suicide and up to 58% of those who die by suicide, do not have any prior mental illness. They are often plagued by overwhelming circumstances, primarily stemming from family discord, breakdown of relationships, sociopolitical and governance-related issues resulting in hopelessness and despair. No one likes to be rejected, everyone wants to count. Everyone needs to be seen, acknowledged and validated, and that is the major problem with Emeka. He feels invisible.

In Nigeria and other areas of Sub-Saharan Africa, widespread addiction to codeine-containing cough medicines have become a major healthcare crisis. Codeine is an Opiate, much like Heroin or Morphine. It is primarily used to treat pain but is also found in some cough medicines. Ironically, its use as an ingredient in cough medicines has been banned in western countries, but that is sadly not the situation in many African countries, and Nigeria appears to be at the forefront of this. Some of the cough medicines are manufactured in Nigeria, and some are imported. Although the Nigerian government has been *"fighting"* it, widespread corruption in the medical field itself, is a major force hampering any progress. There are cases of individuals in the pharmaceutical companies trafficking and selling the cough medicines in huge quantities in the black market. In a BBC.com article in May of 2018, it was reported that the Nigerian government has outlawed the manufacture of this deadly drug, but the fight to abolish it at the ground level is proving to be a major uphill task. It is easily available as we read in the story, and there are no regulations for dosing, hence the ease of addiction.

Dichlorvos or DDVP is 2,2 dichlorovinyl dimethyl phosphate popularly known as *SNIPER*. It is an organophosphate pesticide that was initially banned in some European countries 1998, and was banned across all European Union countries in 2012 due to its high neurotoxicity. Sadly, it is still being exported to third world countries to be used as rat poison. It is an acetylcholinesterase inhibitor affecting nerve conduction and leading to paralysis, low blood pressure, cardiac abnormalities and death within hours of ingestion. Disastrously, in recent years it has gained popularity as a vehicle for suicide amongst Nigerian Youth, mainly because it is easily available. With little to no medical care available to the masses, there is ineffective resuscitation when these victims are found, so death is almost a guarantee when ingested. I remember one of my mom's dogs died after ingesting it. The poison had been sprayed around the house to kill mice.

Homelessness is a common problem of at-risk LGBTQ+ youth. Did you know that 40% of homeless youth in the US are LGBTQ+? They are 120 times more likely to experience homelessness than non-LGBTQ+ youth. I don't have any numbers from Nigeria, but your guess is as good as mine. Ostracization of LGBTQ+ youth is very prevalent in many homes, communities, and religious organizations in most countries. In the LBGTQ+ community, Trans youth are by far at highest risk for suicidal behavior. But LGBTQ+ youth have the highest rate of suicide attempts amongst all youth in the US. Family conflict is the most common cause of all youth homelessness. For these youth in particular, the conflict tends to be over their sexual orientation or gender identity. Very often, life on the street comes with all kinds of dire circumstances, from rape to kidnapping to drug use, and even death. Unfortunately, this is a reality for many of the youth. Luckily, there are lots of non-profit organizations that exist to ensure that they get the help they need. These include: The Trevor Project, True Colors United, The Human Rights Campaign, and now we have a brand-new Trans Lifeline for outreach (877) 565-8860. Below are the 2018 statistics from The LGBTQ+ Youth Report study carried out by the Human Rights Campaign researchers at the University of Connecticut:

- 77% of LGBTQ+ teenagers surveyed report feeling depressed or down over the past week.
- 95% of LGBTQ+ youth report trouble sleeping at night.
- LGBTQ+ youth of color and transgender teenagers experience unique challenges and elevated stress -- only 11% of youth of color surveyed believe their racial or ethnic group is regarded positively in the U.S, and over 50% of trans and gender expansive youth said they can *never* use school restrooms that align with their gender identity.
- More than 70% report feelings of worthlessness and hopelessness in the past week.

- Only 26% say they always feel safe in their school classrooms -- and just 5% say all their teachers and school staff are supportive of LGBTQ+ people.
- 67% report that they've heard family members make negative comments about LGBTQ+ people.
- See resources page below for more info.

Chapter 22

TEENAGE LOVE AND TEENAGE PREGNANCY

"Your future is not ahead of you it is inside of you"

~ Anonymous

Brandie

Hello Dr. Lulu,

My name is Brandie. I am a 16-year-old high school student. I live in Brooklyn, New York. I am writing to tell you about my current dilemma for which I am in need of your help. First a little bit of background about me. My maternal grandparents are Jamaican Immigrants. They moved to the US to find greener pastures after they got married in the mid-1960s. Both my parents were born to immigrant families. My father's parents are Haitian with a long line of ancestors living in the US. My parents were high school sweethearts. They both went to school right here in Brooklyn, on Flatbush avenue where they grew up. We live only one block away from both my grandparents, and most of my aunts and uncles live within walking distance from our apartment complex. I have always had my family around me.

I attend the S.T.A.R early college school at Erasmus, one of the 5 schools within the former Erasmus Hall High school. I love my school. It has a partnership with Brooklyn college, so students are able to take college classes, and I am on the Science, Technology, English, Art and Math (STEAM) track. I plan on attending NYU for my undergraduate studies to major in biomedical engineering. My school curriculum is tight. I am taking Physics, Spanish 3 and English at college level. I get a lot of one-on-one tutoring time with my teachers, so I can stay ahead on my fast track to college. My plan is to keep college as short as possible so my parents don't have to spend too much money on me, and, so I can finish early and start working to make good money and travel the world. As much as I love my family, my plan is to move out of Brooklyn and see what else the world has to offer.

I love to travel, unfortunately, I haven't had much of an opportunity, my parents can't afford it. I am one of 5 children in total, and though my parents work very hard, there is only so much they can do with so many mouths to feed. That is why I am so happy that I am strong academically. Despite a challenging curriculum, I am proud to say that I still find time for some extra-curricular activities. I am told this will help make my resume and college apps more well-rounded and interesting to the fancy colleges out there. I signed up for debate club and I love it. It is

156

helping me with my public speaking skills. I am practicing how to have grace under pressure and critical thinking. For the most part, life is good.

I know, you are wondering why I am writing this letter since everything is so chill, right? Well, wrong. Just like all the *"fake"* happy faces we see on social media, where everyone looks like they never had a bad day in their lives, I have also learned to fake it, or die trying, lol.

You see, last year towards the end of my sophomore year, I met someone. I have had to keep it a secret this entire time because of the particular person that he is. Growing up in a semi- traditional Jamaican family, I know that my grandparents and parents would never approve. The only fair to good thing about my situation is that he is also of Jamaican ancestry. He is a basketball coach at the neighborhood Young Men's Christian Association (YMCA) here on Flatbush avenue. I met him last year when I went for tryouts with some of my friends for the female basketball team. He was coaching the pee wee basketball team that fateful Saturday and it was the most beautiful thing I had ever seen. He, standing at 6ft 6in, and the little people, all way below his kneecaps. He looked so handsome, that I was hooked at first sight. I think I must have performed poorly that afternoon because I was so distracted by him. But somehow, I made the team. One my way out, I felt his eyes boring into my back, so I turned around, and our eyes met. I knew right away that we were going to make history together. Have you ever felt that way, Dr. Lulu?

Have you ever known someone deep in your heart even before you really got to know them?

At practice the next week, he walked up to me and asked my name. My heart was beating so loudly and rapidly, I could have sworn everyone in the gym could hear it! I never responded to his question, I simply asked him his name. *"Sullivan."* And the next thing I knew, we were an item. *A secret item though, because, he is married.* Yes, I hate to say that my first love, my first boyfriend, my first heart throb is a married man. His heart belonged to another woman, and there was nothing I could do about it. I knew better. I knew I had no business hanging around older men, but the joy of the thrill and the excitement of finally having a boyfriend like the rest of my friends was overwhelming and overpowering. If anyone had ever told me that I would be in this predicament, by choice, I would never have believed them.

I was a virgin, but I was happy to give it up to him. He is that good ☺. We have been dating secretly for over a year now, and I am not sure what to do about it. I love him, but he tells me it's not real love. He tells me I will grow up and meet someone else, someone closer to my age. Oh, I forgot to tell you he is 10 years my senior. But I love him anyway. He is so much more mature than all these boys I see on the school campus. He is a real man, not a boy. And I don't know what to do. It looks like the fun part is over for him now that he has my heart, and he is asking me now to stop calling and texting him. He is now telling me the entire thing was a mistake, but it is too late. Not only am I too deep in, I also found out last month, that I am 9 weeks pregnant. I haven't told him. I haven't told anyone. I am only telling you, Dr. Lulu.

My parents are going to kill me if they find out. My whole life is over, my future is forever changed because of this. But that is not all. Last week, when I went to see the doctor, I was told that my blood results came back, and I have *Chlamydia* and *Herpes*. They also mentioned something about my blood type or was it my blood pressure? I can't really remember. I can't believe it. I am in shock. I am so ashamed of what I have done. I am afraid I might die from complications of the pregnancy or the infections. I hear *Herpes* is not curable, does that mean I will have it forever? Could I die from it? Will my blood readings ever become normal?

I have no one to turn to at this time. This is not happening to me. This is not my life. This is not the way I envisioned myself at the tender age of 17 years. I have my entire future ahead of me. My life cannot be over now. Not today, not before I get to go to college, or even graduate from high school. The worst thing is, these days, he avoids me. He won't take my calls. He hasn't been at the gym lately when I stop by like I used to (that was our meetup place). I don't know where he lives, and I don't know where to find him. I can't tell anyone else just yet. I don't know what to do.

I read somewhere that black women hardly ever get depressed, or suicidal, but those are my two companions these days. I feel like a disappointment to my family, my friends, my teachers who have put in a lot of time and effort into teaching me, but mostly, I feel like I have failed myself. I don't know if I can live with this guilt and shame any more. I can't face my beautiful loving family, I can't face my grandmothers, I can't face my cousins and I definitely can't face my parents. I have written them all a long letter explaining everything to them, but I haven't mailed it out yet.

I did some research and found some Paraquat online. Since I was born on March 11, I shall use it on the 11th of this month. I can't imagine living a life as a single mom, or as a school drop-out. I can't imagine bringing a child into this life with the possibility that they might get infected with *Herpes* or worse, end up still born, I hear lots of teen births are stillborn. I will not be able to forgive myself knowing that I caused that. I can't allow myself to do that. I am so confused, and afraid, I don't really know what to do. Please help me!

Brandie.

Dear Brandie,

I completely understand how hard life can seem especially when you are so young and find yourself suddenly stuck, disappointed and abandoned with what seems like nowhere to go. Do please remember as you stated, that you have a loving family, and though you have made a mistake, it is not the end of the world. Normal people like you and I make mistakes every day. We must learn to forgive ourselves and move on, your family still loves you and will most likely be willing to forgive you, because each of them has also made mistakes in the past. What you must do is come clean with them, and hopefully you have learned from this experience. Telling them the truth will certainly lighten your burden. Remember, you have a baby inside of you that needs taking care of. You also need to be well nourished and at a good place mentally so your body can carry your baby to term. I know you are worried about school and the future. All is not lost, you can still carry on with your education, if you choose to. Many-a-teen-mom have gone on to have their babies and live a successful and even famous life (see discussion below).

And yes, to answer your question directly, indeed I have fallen in love like you did before. I met her for only a few moments, and I knew right away, deep in my heart that we would have history together. I was so sure about it, that I called her the next day and she told me that she was also thinking about me. And we have been married since then. So, you see? It is quite normal to fall in love like you did, at first sight, and even live happily ever after! ☺

Nowadays, there are plenty of resources for single moms and their babies (see resources page below). So, there is also no need to worry about you and your baby's future. There is also free health insurance available, in the form of Medicaid for pregnant moms. And most importantly, you are not alone. You need your family, and your family needs you. This is only a bump on the road. I will need you to be kind and understanding to yourself. Remember to practice self-love, self-compassion and self-forgiveness daily. You are worth it.

As for the sexually transmitted infections (STIs) you have been diagnosed with, they are both treatable, and manageable, your doctors will explain it all to you. You might need to hold off on your boyfriend for now and focus on yourself and the baby. I know that might be hard, but let's take a step back and just breathe, it will all be okay in the end, I promise. However, if he decides to come into the picture, that will certainly help you and the baby tremendously, as long as he is willing to be supportive. The first step is to tell your family, so we can get you proper prenatal care which will most likely increase chances of having a safe and healthy pregnancy.

Lastly, please remember, hurting yourself or the baby is never a good route to go. I know you feel trapped right now, hurt and disappointed, but please get rid of the Paraquat. There will be no need for that. I am here for you if you ever need me. I am literally a simple phone call or text away (you can find my cell number and email address on the resources page of this book). Also, if you need me to speak to your parents on your behalf, I shall be only too willing to help. Just please reach out. For all you know one of your other family members might have had similar circumstances but have never talked about it, and you might be the reason it will all come back to the surface. Again, please reach out to someone, soon.

Loving you so much, and routing for you, and the baby 😊

Yours in love,

Dr. Lulu

Discussion

The truth is, teen pregnancy, though at an all-time low in recent years in the US, is still very prevalent compared to other developed countries. Risk factors for teen pregnancy include: lack of education and understanding about their bodies and the interplay between sex and pregnancy, low household income, sexual abuse, low self-esteem, sex at a young age, drug and alcohol use, peer pressure, dating older men, sexually active friends, family history of teen pregnancies, significant family conflict, single parent home, poor parental supervision, and the welfare/foster care system. Though these factors tend to increase the chances of teen pregnancies, there are a great majority of teens who don' fit this mold who also get pregnant. However, our teen Brandie, does have a few of the risk factors listed above. While most parents would like to think their teens will never have unprotected sex during adolescence, it can happen in any family.

Numerous articles have been written and rewritten on the effects and complications of teen pregnancy. There is no doubt that it definitely complicates an already really challenging time in their life. But it is doable, and many former teen moms have gone on to become very successful women. That being said, studies have shown that teen pregnancies often predispose moms to preeclampsia, preterm labor, and other complications especially if the pregnancy is not supervised. On the long term, teen pregnancies lead to increased school dropout, and offspring of teen pregnancies also have a high incidence of school dropouts. Their offspring also have more health problems, more incarceration, more unemployment, and in turn become teen parents themselves. There are obviously many cases of products of teen pregnancies that have gone on to do very well and succeed in life, one such person is me, Dr. Lulu. Yes, my mother had me at 19 years of age. Bet you didn't know that! 😊 Writing this book actually made me come to terms with it, and for that, I am eternally grateful. Yes, she was happily married, and my father was a budding Nigerian Air Force officer (and not a teen), but my mother was a teenager. Unfortunately, for some reason, we nearly always focus only on negative outcomes…

With tender loving care from parents and trusted adults in the teen's lives, most teen moms do well. The teen-mom's significant other, whether himself a teen, or not (as in Brandie's case), also needs to be involved in the entire pregnancy, birth and child rearing process. His presence and support are pivotal, and result in improved outcomes both for the mother and their offspring. Specifically, his presence will improve the offspring's language skills, cognitive skills and overall behavior.

The decline in teen pregnancy rate in the US has been praised as one of the major achievements in women's health in the last 70 years! The decline crosses all races and ethnicities. Some of the possible reasons are, increased education about birth control and safe sex or abstinence, decreased sexual activity amongst teens, and increased use of birth control. This was a welcome surprise for me because we are all aware of the near glamorization of teen pregnancy on TV shows these days. It appears more and more teens are becoming aware of the consequences of teen pregnancy and becoming more proactive and intentional about it. As a pediatrician and parent coach, my best advice to parents would be to talk about sex, abstinence, and birth control openly with your teens, whether they are boys or girls. Give them a truthful narrative about it all. Ensure they fully understand the facts and repercussions of unplanned pregnancies. Though this story is about a female teenager, there are teen fathers out there as well, and their stories are largely untold... Note to self (hint, hint ☺).

Most parents/families don't believe they will ever have to deal with a teen pregnancy, especially those with sons. But teen sexual activity is still extremely prevalent, and more teen boys report sexual activity and at an earlier age, than teen girls. ***It is therefore imperative that you, parents start early to have <u>ongoing</u> conversations about sex with your teens***. Don't ever assume they are not interested in sex. With the excessive use of social media and everyone owning a smart phone, sexting, and pornography have now become a huge issue. Don't be blindsided, please be proactive and non-judgmental.

Have a round table discussion about sex in your homes and give them the necessary tools they might need. I keep it very real with my boys. They know I don't approve of sex in high school, but I still remind them as often as I can and ask them open-ended questions. I have one son in high school as I type these words, and he knows the drill. I give the two in college bags of condoms each time they go back to school, because I want to ensure they have one less thing to worry about if, and when the urge arises. I have an open-door policy in my home, my sons know they can come to me with any issues they might have, and they will not be judged. I might get dramatic (like most West African moms), but it is all in good faith 😊.

In my first book, I discuss the need for honesty in the home, and I encourage parents to have open and truthful discussions with their children. Share your own stories with them, tell them about your mistakes if you can, the more real you show them you are, the better. One thing that I have always done is keep my boys active in and out of school. I shall discuss some of those activities later in this book. If all else fails, and you don't really know what to say or how to go about having the conversation, take your teen to their doctor, tell the doctor what you are needing them to do, and allow them to be seen alone. Sometimes, teens who are afraid or uncomfortable with asking their parents questions about sex or contraception will be more willing to discuss the subject with a (neutral, trusted) medical professional. You must also ensure you don't get too nosey and ask them embarrassing questions afterwards 😊.

Chapter 23

STOLEN INNOCENCE AND HIV INFECTION

"Give a child love, laughter and peace, not AIDS."

~ Nelson Mandela

Kesi

Hello Dr. Lulu,

My name is Kesi, I am from Kenya in East Africa. My native language is Kikuyu, but I speak fluent KiSwahili (Swahili). Though I currently live in the outskirts of Nairobi, our nation's capital, my family and I are originally from Watamu, a popular beach village-turned small town along the coast of the Indian ocean. My father died a few months after I was born, it is uncertain, but rumors have it that he died of AIDs. My name Kesi, means *"born during a time of great trouble for my father."* I believe I was given that name as a reminder of my dad's illness. When I turned 3, I am told that my mother also took ill, but she was not sick for a very long time, she died after a few short months, leaving me and my elder sister orphans. Being an orphan in my part of the world is not a rarity, many of our parents contract HIV and die due to lack of access to the scant medical resources that we have.

After our mom's death, my sister and I went to live with our aunt whose husband had also recently passed away, and even though she was sick herself, she refused to let us go live in the orphanage. She had no children of her own, so my sister and I filled a void for her. She was very kind to us, one of the kindest people I ever knew at that time. She would tell us stories about her childhood, growing up in the village with no running water, and having to walk up to 10 kilometers (about 6miles) round trip to the well to fetch water. She taught us how to wrap cloth properly to balance a bucket of water on our heads. She made us promise to stay in school, get an education and get as far away as we could from our little town, travel and see the world. And she made us promise to always be there for each other, take care of each other, and support each other. We promised her we would. But by the time I entered elementary school at the age of 7, my aunt passed away. It is also rumored that she had AIDS. My sister (who was 9 years old at that time), and I eventually had to leave her home and go live in the nearby orphanage, one of three in Watamu. Life in the orphanage could have been much worse had I not had my sister, my guardian angel, with me.

When she turned 12, she was married off by some of our distant relatives (whom we had never met) to a 38-year-old already married man who lived in another village more than 100km away from our orphanage. She was not even allowed to complete school. The proprietors of the orphanage explained that she had to get married so she could have a better future. I suspect it was a business deal. I remember the look of defiance in my sister's eyes the night before she was to leave. She swore she was going to run away. She asked me to stay behind, that she would come back for me. I didn't know what to do, I begged her to let me go with her, but she refused. She left the next morning at the crack of dawn with a tiny backpack.

I have never seen her again.

Life for me after my sister's departure has been nothing short of terrible. I am now 15 years old, and already had a child, even though he died, he was still my baby. I don't even know how I got to this point. One thing led to another and suddenly I found myself pregnant with my first child at the age of 13. The whole thing happened so fast, and I can't believe this is now my reality.

It all started when I turned 10. Our orphanage burned down, and many of the children living there had to be relocated. I, along with 5 others were sent to live in a larger orphanage in Nairobi. It was run by expatriates, assisted by local help. One of them, a 24-year-old man, Steven, took a liking to me immediately. He would bring me sweets and little gifts and told me he would take care of me. I was always thankful and actually grateful that God had sent me another angel to take care of me. So, I allowed him to be *"nice"* to me. This went on for a couple of years. Everything was looking good, and I was beginning to settle into my life there.

One day I was sick with malaria, so I had to stay indoors while the other kids went to school. Steven came into my bedroom to visit me and brought me some bread and oranges. I thanked him and put it away, I wasn't *really* hungry. He sat down and asked me how I was feeling. I responded that I was taking my medicine, but my mouth was bitter, and food did not taste right, and asked him if I could eat the food much later. He said, *"sure eat it whenever you like."* *"I hope you feel better soon, so you can go back to school."* I said, *"thank you."* He then got up and started walking towards the door, so I laid back on the bed, closed my eyes and turned around to sleep. The next thing I felt was his large body on top of me. He pressed me really hard against the thin threadbare mattress and covered my mouth with one hand. I couldn't breathe, I couldn't shout, I couldn't move, but my entire body could feel every spring on my bed frame... And his body on mine. Then very quickly, as if in a rush to get something done with an urgency, he took my virginity.

I couldn't believe what had happened, I just laid there, motionless. I was scared and barely able to breathe. I was confused and somehow, I was ashamed. I was in pain and I was bleeding. I was sick, sick to my stomach. I was nauseous and my head was spinning around. I wasn't sure if my malarial fever was back or if it was from what had just happened. My heart was pounding, my head was hurting, and my whole body ached inside and out. I was shivering, my thin blanket could not keep me warm enough. Then it hit me... I had just been raped! That was when he got up, cleaned himself up with my tees-shirt, turned around and left the room without a word.

As the hours turned to days, and days turned to weeks, I couldn't tell anybody. He told me I would be sent away if I told anyone. So, I kept my mouth shut knowing fully well that what he had done was wrong. I couldn't understand the whole thing. I thought he was nice. I thought he was an angel sent from heaven to take care of me. I had actually grown to like him and appreciate his *"kindness and friendship"* towards me all those months before. Several weeks later I started experiencing morning sickness, and we eventually discovered that I was pregnant. I told them who had done it, and even though I was only 12yr old, I was sent away from the orphanage, because pregnancy is not condoned there, and the worst thing is, he was still working there as a caretaker.

One of the expatriate proprietors kindly allowed me to stay in her home until the baby was born, but he was born very premature and he was a stillbirth. After my delivery, I pleaded with her to allow me stay on. I told her I had nowhere to go. I promised her I would be no trouble. I would help cook, clean, and keep the house for her. She finally allowed me to stay on and work for her as a house help, and that has been working out well.

A few months after my baby's birth, I got sick. I developed a weird rash, and I kept running fevers. Then I started losing weight, then my skin became ashen. Then my eyes became hollow and my hair was falling out. I had diarrhea every day, and the worst ulcers in my mouth. I felt terrible and begged my boss lady to please take me to the doctor. When I was finally taken to the hospital, the doctors told us I have HIV. Luckily, my CD4+ count was not terribly low, but it was low enough for my symptoms to be manifesting. They quickly put me on an antiretroviral regimen of many, many pills. Some for the virus, some for my symptoms, and others for the side effects of all the others. In all, I was given about 8 different pills to take every day.

I have been living with this illness for over 2 years now, and I am tired. I don't see myself with a bright future or any future at all. I am alone in the world. I wish I could find my sister to tell her. I wish I had a mother or a father to tell. I wish I had someone to love me, or even hug me on my lonely days, but there isn't. I am truly tired. These days, I hardly take my medicine. I want to die. I can't live in this life anymore. No parents, no sister, no baby, no one but me. I can't go to school because pregnant girls are not allowed to attend school. I don't have any friends. I don't want to live a life like that, I probably will never get married or have any more children. I am only telling you, Dr. Lulu, so at least someone knows. But I have no hope in this life anymore.

Beloved,

One can only begin to imagine what it takes to be a child like you. So strong, so powerful, so courageous! In less than 2 decades you have been through so much pain and so much sadness, more than most adults can endure in their lifetime. Life has indeed thrown you some serious curve balls and one can only imagine how you are able to cope.

I completely understand why you would no longer wish to exist in this world. To be so young and to have experienced such trauma as a child is unimaginable. The death of both parents, the loss of your only sister, a rape and the birth of a stillborn child, now culminating with a diagnosis of HIV infection? I can only imagine the deep sorrow your heart has felt.

I will start by saying again, how brave you are to have survived such heartache and loss. Please know that even by writing this letter to me, you are already on your road to recovery. I know it might not feel that way, but believe me, you are! You might not know just how courageous you are for wanting to share your story with me and the rest of the world, but I am here to tell you that your story, sad as it is will give many people hope. Many of us that think we have it bad, those of us that feel like giving up for far lesser situations will hear your story and be encouraged by it.

The first thing I would advise you to do is to continue taking your medicines daily, you need them to stay strong physically. As for your emotional health, I see that you are quite a good storyteller, you will make a great author, you are already on your way. Continue to write your thoughts and feelings down. It is often a therapeutic thing. It will help you with your healing.

I am happy to know that you have a safe place to stay, that is awesome! We shall have to get you back into school to complete your education so your future will be that much brighter. The diagnosis of HIV is no longer the *"death sentence"* it used to be many moons ago. There are many new updated medications available these days to keep you as healthy as anyone else.

What would you like to be when you grow up? Any dreams? I see you becoming a great author, speaker, and even mentor. We might have to find a support group of other teens like you that will help strengthen you when your spirits are down. You can learn a craft, or you can get a job or volunteer by helping other children at an orphanage. Don't worry about the future for now, let us take it one day at a time.

Can you enroll with the DREAMS project? Or the Befrienders organization? Have you heard about them? I discuss their services briefly below. I contacted the Befrienders organization while working on this book, I have information on how to reach them, it will be in the resources section. They were very open to collaborating with me and my cause. One of their leaders is actually going to be a guest on my podcast in the near future. But for now, let's get you signed up with either, or both organizations to start getting you much needed assistance and the services of a supportive, trusted and reliable community to lean on.

Sending you lots of love, light and strength,

Dr. Lulu.

Discussion

I wish I could honestly say Kesi's case is different or unique. Unfortunately, I can't. While doing the research for this book, I came across some horrendous statistics and even more horrendous practices in certain parts of Africa that simply put, gave me sleepless nights for days.

Let's take a closer look: Sub-Saharan Africa is home to 24 of the 25 countries with the world's highest HIV infection rates. Kenya ranks third in the continent of Africa, next to Uganda and Mozambique. In 2018, an estimated 1.6M Kenyans are living with HIV infection. The prevalence rate for ages 15-49 is 4.7%, with 46,000 new infections and 25,000 AIDS-related deaths. You and I know these numbers are only those counted right? The majority of those in the rural areas are often not counted, or due to stigma, many don't volunteer their status, or simply don't know.

The population at highest risk for infections include men having sex with men, sex workers, drug users and women/girls. There is a high percentage of babies born infected with HIV, either because their moms' status was unknown during the pregnancy, or because she didn't take any antiretroviral treatment like she was supposed to. Child rape and female sexual exploitation is extremely rampant in this part of the world, partially due to poverty and unemployment, but also due to certain ancient rituals.

Kenya unfortunately, is one of the countries that still practices *"cleansing rituals"*. Sexual cleansing, referred to as *"Kusasa Funbi"* is popular in Kenya, Malawi and other East African and Southern African countries. It involves subjecting pubertal girls or widows to unprotected sex with a pre-selected sex worker known as a *"Hyena"*. Though reportedly outlawed, it is still commonplace and has played a huge role in the spread of HIV, other STIs, and unplanned pregnancies.

175

The ritual is supposed to cleanse participants of unwanted spirits! Seriously? In 2019? Wow! And unbelievably, the Hyena could have sex with hundreds of these poor girls during the cleansing season, with absolutely no protection! Huh! ☹ This was bad enough...

But the worst ritual of all, which I believe our Kesi was a victim of, is the ritual of *"virgin cleansing"*. This is a practice whereby HIV positive men rape virgin-girls as young as 9months old, because it is believed that the act will cure them of their HIV! Can you believe this? The reasoning is that the blood produced by raping a virgin will cleanse the virus from the infected person's blood. ***The younger the virgin, the better the cure.*** This has led to an epidemic of rapes by infected males, with the consequent widespread infection of innocent girls. Sadly, this only perpetuates the prevalence of the disease, causing unnecessary hardship and death. To compound the situation, pregnant teens are often stigmatized, ostracized and not allowed to return to school.

The African continent has the highest adolescent pregnancy rates in the world, according to the United Nations. Every year, thousands of girls become pregnant at the time when they should be learning history, algebra, and life skills. Adolescent girls who have early, and unintended pregnancies face many social and financial barriers to continuing with formal education. Many become single mothers as young as age 9, with the tough responsibility of raising a child. Many die during childbirth. Those that survive and are old enough end up taking jobs as sex workers, further worsening their situations.

In 2013, all the countries that make up the African Union (AU) adopted Agenda 2063, a continent-wide economic and social development strategy. Under this strategy, African governments committed to build Africa's *"human capital,"* which it terms *"its most precious resource,"* through sustained investments in education, including *"elimination of gender disparities at all levels of education."* Though these laws are in place, they are largely not effective, and school dropout rates are still alarmingly high for affected girls.

Suicide rates in Kenyan men are nearly thrice those of the women, but more women attempt suicide than men. Many of these women lack proper psychosocial support systems, and many have a hard time getting much needed medical care for themselves and their children. The absent father syndrome (as mentioned earlier) is very prevalent in most of East and Southern Africa, and that has its own ills. Many children, particularly girls, grow up without the necessary input from a paternal figure, leading to widespread unchecked exploitation by other men, and the consequences are dire. These girls for the most part have been failed by the adults who were supposed to be their custodians.

Like Kesi, many HIV positive adolescents find themselves in a near hopeless situation, there is an extreme lack of government protection against these sexual rituals. Although there seems to be a heightened awareness of HIV and AIDS in Kenya, the high levels of discrimination, stigma and poverty are major roadblocks when it comes to obtaining proper access to services. Hence there is a proliferation of the practice of *"slow suicide,"* a phenomenon characterized by a prolonged period of self-abuse and harmful behavior which may result in loss of life. In the case of some HIV-positive people, the process involves not taking their medicines in order to speed up the process of inevitable death.

In 2014, Kenya and nine other East African countries were enrolled in the Determined, Resilient, Empowered, AIDS-free, Mentored, and Safe (DREAMS) project. An initiative by the US President's Emergency Plan for AIDS Relief (PEPFAR) to help with HIV prevention and gender-based violence among young women and girls who make up more than half of all new HIV infections. They offer education and training and rehabilitative services. Though they only enroll those that are HIV negative, they do refer those that are HIV positive to treatment centers and ensure they receive appropriate treatment and medications. They also assist with counseling and other forms of assistance that their enrollees need. Though our Kesi will not qualify for all the services they offer, enrolling with them would be a good place to start.

Another great humanitarian resource for mental health patients in Kenya is the all-volunteer Befrienders charitable organization which focuses on suicide prevention by offering emotional support to those who may be in distress. Their mission, like mine is creating awareness for, and providing much needed help for suicide prevention within communities for those in danger. It is so far, the only organization in Kenya with a specific focus on suicide prevention.

Chapter 24

GENERATIONAL TRAUMA

AND

SUICIDE CLUSTERS

"Sometimes even to live is an act of courage."

~ Lucius Annaeus Seneca

Zaltana

Dear Dr. Lulu,

I am a 19-year-old Apache Native American Indian, my name is Zaltana. It means *"high mountain"*. I was born in the Fort Apache Indian Reservation in Arizona, United States. My reservation encompasses parts of Navajo, Gila and Apache counties. It is home to the federally recognized White Mountain Apache Tribe of the Fort Apache Reservation, a Western Apache tribe. There are many types and tribes of Apache Indians, and once upon a time I promised myself I would ensure the world learns about our culture and respects our differences. I am hoping to go to college this fall to study psychology

179

as my prerequisite for medicine, so I can come back and work in my community. We barely have any social services here, and our people die every day as a result.

I was named in honor of my great grandfather. Legend has it that he was a great Apache warrior, who went up to the White Mountain to fight and conquer invaders, both foreigners and other Indian tribes. He was very active in the Apache wars, and it is rumored that he was involved in getting Geronimo to surrender peacefully. I am very proud of my history and my heritage. I am proud that I come from a long line of warriors and survivors, but unfortunately, I am writing to tell you that the past few years have been extremely challenging for me.

Our communities have been ridden with all sorts of social problems. Top of which are: alcoholism and drug abuse, bullying, violence, high unemployment and school dropout rates, and high levels of poverty and deprivation. My friends and I are a resilient group, we are searching for solutions to some of these problems, but it is quite difficult because of our history of trauma and genocide. Hardly one semester passes in school when one of us does not have a funeral, usually of a loved one, and very often they are not even 30 years of age.

Since my father died by suicide a few years ago, my mother has never been the same. She is currently battling alcoholism and depression. As a result, my younger sisters and I are currently living with our maternal grandparents. Thankfully, my grandparents and other extended family members are a solid support network for us. They teach us our traditions and help keep our pasts alive, they are the connection to our ancestors, and I really appreciate that. Life in general is not too hard for me, but every now and again, I hear one of my sisters crying and saying they miss our mom. Due to my mother's illness and struggles with alcohol, I made a vow to myself to avoid drinking at all costs and I have kept it so far. I don't know if you know this, but there is a high prevalence of alcoholism amongst native Americans as a whole.

A few months ago, one of my dearest high school friends died from an overdose of methamphetamine, which has recently become an epidemic around here. We are still not sure if it was accidental or not, she had been going through a lot with her boyfriend who was very physically abusive. Right before she died, she had confided in me that she might be pregnant, I didn't exactly know what to say, what to do, or how to help her. I know that was a huge source of concern for her because like most of us, her parents are very poor. And though teen pregnancy rates are high in our community, it is difficult and challenging. She was very worried about possibly having to drop out of school, because there are no jobs around here even for those that graduate, and she did not feel supported by her boyfriend.

As the *"man of the house,"* I have a heavy burden of responsibility on my hands and I am getting a bit overwhelmed by them. Just this past week, there was another suicide in our community. A young man, only 17 years old, he died from a single self-inflicted gunshot wound to the head. I went to high school with his older brother and I knew his family well. This happened in the wake of the burial of yet another community member this past Spring, he also died by suicide, his family returned from an outing to find him hanging from a tree in their backyard.

I am stressed out and could use any kind of advice you can offer. I am not entirely sure which way to go, I am concerned about going off to college and leaving my siblings behind. I know they will be in good hands, but I still worry. I am concerned that my mother's illness might get worse while I am away at college. I am not currently dating, so, that is one less thing to worry about. But my grandparents are old, and life is so hard, the government promises resources, but never deliver.

Things are really tough for me. I am not sure what to do. My biggest issue is how to fend for my family. I am very likely going to get a college scholarship because my grades are great, and we have access to many government funded grants and scholarships that I have applied for, so that is not an issue. But sometimes I wake up in the middle of the night covered in cold sweats with palpitations. I am not sure why. I also have a hard time falling asleep most nights, because my mind is always racing and wondering where help will come from. I put up a brave front for my family, but I am truly dying inside. I need your help Dr. Lulu, before I lose my mind.

Please, can you help me? Dr. Lulu? I am open to any reasonable suggestions on how to balance it all: life at school, my siblings, my grandparents, my ailing mom, my immediate future, my emotional needs and my friends and community as well.

Thank you so kindly.

Zaltana

Dearest Child,

I am unable to articulate in words what I am feeling as I read your letter. Honestly, my heart is racing right next to yours. Let me start by applauding you for being the *"man of the house"* and handling it so well (at least to the outside world). You are indeed a blessing to your siblings, your grandparents, your family and the community in general. What a sweet thing to want to become a doctor when you grow up to give back to the community and help in that way! I am already so very proud of you. I know your grandfather and your dad are also smiling down on you and cheering you on. Being an Igbo woman, I am superstitious like that. My tribe, not unlike yours, also believe in reincarnation, and in the power of ancestral spirits and their presence amongst us. I know yours are raining blessings down on you from the great beyond.

I am so sorry about the terrible losses you have endured at such a tender age in such quick succession. I can only imagine life without your friend, your father, and then to add to these, your ailing mom. By the way, how is her depression? Is she getting any treatment and support for her alcoholism? Is she responding well? Are there such services available in your community? My guess is she might not be getting adequate help based on the tone of your letter, re: paucity of services. Hmmm, such a shame that the US government treats its Indigenous populations like that.

How are you doing emotionally? You sound like you are having some attacks of anxiety, and rightfully so. It is a lot of weight for anyone to carry. Are you able to get any kind of therapy or counseling? Is there an ability to have you and your friends get mental health evaluations to assess your needs? It would be great to have you speak with someone about your concerns, a counselor, a therapist, a doctor, or even a teen support group that you can join, and if there isn't one, maybe you could start one! Why not? That's what they say right? If you need something and you can't find it, start your own. That could give you something to occupy your time while you wait for college, as well as give you something to do when you return home on vacations. Your sisters can also join in, even though you didn't mention their ages, I know that sitting around peers and sharing their fears and concerns would certainly help.

How about we start with those ideas for now? I also meant to add journaling to the list, that always helps me feel better. I journal literally daily. It gives me something to look forward to and helps me stay accountable to myself and is a reminder to be grateful for the good things that happens each day. Try that, you might even like it 😊

You could also try some breathing exercises at bedtime. There are numerous apps available on your smart phone for that. One that I have tried myself is the Breath2Relax app. There is also meditation, which many people swear by. An easy self-guided method is the 4-7-8 breathing technique. Very simple and relaxing. It helps my patients with anxiety get re-centered and reset when they start getting exacerbations.

So, how about you start working on these suggestions, and I will check back in with you in a couple of weeks? Until then, keep being strong and keep being an inspiration.

Peace Still.

Dr. Lulu.

Discussion

As mentioned in part one of this book, American Indian/Alaskan Native (AI/AN) adolescents and young adults, have alarmingly high suicide rates in the US. It is the second leading cause of death for AI/AN youth, but this group of teens also have the highest suicide rates of any race in the US. Depending on what study you read, they are also at greater risk for suicide attempts and suicide contagion than their peers of other races, and other age groups. Suicide clusters can occur within close-knit, rural AI/AN communities and the effects can be devastating to everyone, youth, families, and the communities. Adolescents and the youth from these communities have the highest rates of suicide contagion. Researchers note that one of the most distinctive features about clusters of suicide attempts and suicides is that they occur almost exclusively among teenagers. Direct and indirect exposure to suicidal behavior has been shown to lead to an increase in suicidal behavior in persons at risk for suicide, usually adolescents and young adults, much like Zaltana. Some reports have shown up to 100 suicides among young AI/AN in communities over short periods of time.

Experts who study Native American suicide patterns have blamed a range of societal ills for their abnormally high numbers. These include: high rates of poverty, substance abuse, unemployment, geographical isolation, generations of what I call *"tribal trauma"* from, and following mass genocide, discrimination and racism, disrupted family units, previous suicide attempt(s), access to lethal means, exposure to others who have died by suicide, physical or sexual abuse, barriers to care, high rates of alcohol and drug use, interpersonal violence and even government-forced boarding schools. Difficulty with access to mental healthcare is also a major reason.

Understandably, there is still lingering distrust of the government by some tribes, from years of disappointments and maltreatment, which further worsens the situation. Lack of understanding and lack of respect of Native American customs by mainstream America is often also an obstacle in communication and progress. Many of the tribes are protective of their customs and insist on continuing their traditional practices, which might sometimes be in direct conflict with orthodox practices, further driving the wedge and worsening an already dismal state of affairs. Though more studies need to be done, the suggestions put forward to help prevent or ameliorate the suicide crisis among young native Americans by the U.S. Department of Health and Human Services (HHS) Office of the Surgeon General and National Action Alliance for Suicide Prevention include:

~ A Community Plan for the Prevention and Containment of Suicide Clusters which should be in place well before the suicides occur.

~ Preventing intentional or unintentional traumatic deaths among the youth, and promotion of health recovery within the community.

~ Screening of high-risk individuals in order to prevent suicide clusters from happening and or spreading.

~ Ensuring that all sectors of the community (e.g. public health, mental health, education, local government, clergy, parent groups, the media, community organizations) are involved in planning and implementing the prevention and response effort.

~ Individual and group counseling for affected communities and peers.

~ Responsible media reporting of the suicides to prevent clusters.

Chapter 25

ERASED BOYHOOD AND HELPLESSNESS

"If you can BELIEVE it, you can BE it."

~ Dr. Lulu

Oumar Muhammad

Dear Dr. Lulu,

My name is Oumar Muhamad. I am from Yemen. I would like to write to you about my current situation. 4 years ago, when I was only 10 years old, a civil war broke out in my country. It is still on-going. I am writing you from my home in Yemen. I live in a southern town called Taiz where on a daily basis, boys (some as young as 10 years old) are being recruited, kidnapped or sometimes sold into war.

I was recruited along with three of my cousins by the Houthis, the Iranian-allied Yemeni group fighting against the Saudi-backed forces. I am the first from my immediate family to go to war. They offered my parents a lot of money, the equivalent of $150, in exchange for my service. They promised to pay more when we arrive at the war camps and training begins. My mother had initially objected to it, but my father and the other men in my family over-ruled her objections. We are poor and desperate for money for food. I remember returning from school that day and noticing my mother's eyes were red and swollen like she had been crying for a while. She told me it was nothing important when I asked her why she was teary-eyed. I later found out that night when my dad came into the tiny bedroom that I share with my two younger brothers to tell me.

I didn't know how to feel that night. I was overcome with fear and anxiety, but my father hugged me and assured me everything was going to be okay. He asked me to be brave and do this service for my country. In Yemen the child is only a child until 12, and then he becomes a man. The society thinks very highly of children who carry arms. My father told me I would not be alone, that I would have my three cousins with me. My brothers are 8 and 9, so I guess they are too young. The rest of that night and the days and nights that followed have been a blur. I vaguely remember my mother moping around the house. My brothers have been very inquisitive, they ask me all sorts of questions, of which I know no answers. As for my father, he too is afraid, I can sense it, but he has never shown it, he puts on a brave face and acts like everything is fine. *"You will go and return before you know it."* He consoled. But I can feel he doesn't really know or understand what is about to happen. I don't either. I have heard stories of boys and men that

190

went to war and never came back. Some come back really hurt, with no hands or no legs. A few come back, appear normal on the outside, but the light in their eyes are switched off. I have always prayed it would never be my turn. I have always hoped the war would be over before I am old enough. I have always hoped…

I don't really know how I was picked to go. Did my father make arrangements with these people? Was this duty meant for someone else? But my siblings are all too young…Who then could it be? Why me? I know we are poor, but I thought we were happy. I enjoy playing with my brothers, and I always do my best to help around the house. I am good at school and respectful to my parents and elders. I faithfully perform my ablution and say my prayers daily like I should. So, again, I ask, why me? I want to become an engineer when I grow up, so I can help rebuild the towns and cities that have been ravaged by war. Am I going to live long enough to achieve my dreams? Will I ever be the same when/if I return from this war? What if I don't make it back, or come back severely injured? How much is my life worth? Even if I do return and wish to pursue my dreams, there is very little education and not much to do here since the war. Is Allah really out there? If He is, why does He allow this? Why is the good Prophet Mohammed not interceding for me? Why am I not receiving answers to my prayers?

As I prepare to leave for training tomorrow, I don't know how to feel, I don't know what to say. I am so scared. I cry every night, but by day I must put on a brave face. My own mother avoids looking into my eyes when I see her. She is almost avoiding me.

As I go to bed for the last time as a child, in my father's house, I pray to Allah again, as I have done daily for the past several weeks and months. I plead with Him to let me die in my sleep, I don't wish to wake up in the morning, but I know I will, and I know I must go, nothing can stop it now. I just wanted you to know.

Thank you.

Oumar

Beloved Oumar,

It is with tears that I read your letter. I too have a 15-year-old son, and I can't even begin to imagine sending him to war, or what I would be doing if he had to go to war at this age. Life has truly dealt you a heavy hand. ☹

I was born in the late 1960s, 1969 to be exact. My country Nigeria was just ending its civil war at that time. I am Igbo by tribe, and yes, my family and I were Biafrans. Some people refer to that war as the Biafran war, or the Nigerian civil war. My father fought in the war as a foot soldier, and my mother was a fire fighter. In a sense, I too was involved in the war through my parents. I personally have never liked war. I don't even like to watch war movies or war documentaries. Unfortunately, I have also never really sat down to ask my parents about their experiences in the war. I know that my people as a tribe are still dealing with the aftermath of that war, over half a century later. So, I hope you can understand why it might be very difficult for me to give advice to you.

192

I wish there was good news I could share with you about your present predicament. I have looked around but the only good thing I can find so far is that you will be in the company of your cousins, for all its worth. And you have your dreams for a better Yemen, which you will *Insha Allah* help to rebuild. I remember a few years ago, hearing my own mother lamenting about the atrocities being committed in Yemen, I half-listened to her back then because of my aversion for war. But I can't run any more, your letter has made me face my fears and my ideations head-on. Thank you for helping me understand what she meant all those years ago.

My prayer is that you don't get hurt and you don't get too emotionally traumatized. But the sad news is you and many of those boys that will fight bravely beside you have already been severely traumatized. The emotional toll on your psyche is already overwhelming. Indeed, you will go as a boy and return as a man. I can only imagine the sights that you will see, the thoughts that you will have, the dreams you will dream and the pain and sadness and fear that will accompany you as you face a very dangerous and uncertain future.

Nothing I say can take those away. I know of grown men who have been at war, who still suffer the horrific consequences to this day. I can only imagine that your experiences will be that much worse, being a mere child and going through so much hardship. However, there is hope. I read about a rehabilitative center for boys who have been child soldiers that is run by the Saudi Arabian government. According to the Saudi press agency, children receive psychological treatment and education to help them recover from their ordeal and integrate back into society. It helps boys return to a semblance of a normal life. It is part of King Salman's Humanitarian Aid and Relief Center's humanitarian project. The center is called *KSRelief* Center and they plan to rehabilitate up to 2000 boy soldiers. I don't know how you would qualify for it, or even if it would still be available when your tour of duty is over, but it is certainly a good start for kids like you who have been recruited by the Houthis.

Hopefully, the warring factions will come to their senses and realize the effects of their obstinacy on innocent people's lives, especially the minors. One can only pray the near future will bring an end to the war for your sake and the sake of all the other children suffering such a life. Do you know if there will be mental healthcare services available for you when you get home? I know that the doctors will take good care of your physical ailments and injuries if any, but what of the mental and emotional care you and your family will need? Is anyone going to take care of that?

I do have some interesting news though. I looked up the meaning of your name, Oumar. It means *"a populous, flourishing, long-lived eloquent speaker."* I know you have been asking the universe for the reason you were *"picked"* to fight this war. The answer might very well lie in your name. You are a natural born leader and destined for greatness *Insha Allah.* Just stay dreaming and believing and you will return, and you will fulfil your destiny to help rebuild your country 😊.

As I end this letter, I wish I wouldn't. I wish I could do more, or say more, but I can't.

Please take good care of yourself. If you have a journal, write in it every day. Keep hope alive. Believe with all your heart that you *can and will* come back. You will be whatever you are destined to be, but I want you to first think it, then want it, then believe it, and it will all be yours...

Look out for your cousins and remain brave. Until I hear back from you, stay positive.

Yours in prayers and hope,

Dr. Lulu.

Discussion

Regarded by some as the *"most corrupt country in the Arab world,"* Yemen, is the second largest country in the Arabian Peninsula. It is bordered in the north by Saudi Arabia, and in the East by Oman. Its capital city of Sana'a has been under Houthi rebel control since February 2015, and the United Nations has reported that Yemen is the country with the most people in need of humanitarian aid in the world, with 24.1 million people in need.

The war in Yemen has been described as the world's worst humanitarian tragedy in recent history, with both factions (A Saudi Arabia-led coalition with the United Arab Emirates (UAE), and

Ansar Allah, aka The Houthis, a Yemeni and (mostly) Iran-backed militia) being involved in child-soldier-recruitment in spite of denials from both sides, and denouncement by the United Nations. The Saudis are largely backed by the United States. What began as a small conflict between a northern Yemeni group of rebels and the then president, Ali Abdullah Saleh as a result of alleged massive financial corruption and economic discrimination of the north has now grown into nearly 5 years of conflict, civil, religious and political unrest with hundreds of thousands of casualties on both sides, and no end in sight.

Unfortunately, both sides have recruited tens of thousands of child soldiers (and counting) over the course of the war. Many reports have documented that some of these children are as young as 8-10 years old. They are often coerced by the soldiers with promises of payment of salaries. Many are abducted, and many more are tricked by the soldiers by asking them to help bury the dead or other non-combat errands, and then they are trapped and sent to the war training camps. Children are readily recruited from orphanages, and schools (some are given passing grades in their classes if they enlist). However, there are also boy soldiers like our Oumar, whose families freely enlist into the army to fight, in order to assist with much needed funds for day to day basics like food and medicine to help their family. Salaries are promised only to families whose children are willing to fight, and some families are even forced to celebrate their children's martyrdom if they die in combat ☹.

All of these children are robbed of their innocence and most do not return, but for those who do, life is never the same. They return a different person than the one who left. ***Consequently, there is erasure of their boyhood and destruction of their manhood.***

Another part of the world where boy soldiers are being recruited for this war is Darfur, Sudan. Although they have vehemently denied it, the Saudi-led coalition has been repeatedly accused of recruiting thousands of boys to fight this war. The Saudis have used their vast oil wealth to outsource the war, mainly by hiring what Sudanese soldiers say are tens of thousands of desperate survivors of the conflict in Darfur to fight. Sudan which has been ravaged by their own internal conflicts and civil war (which just ended less than a decade ago, and left millions dead, displaced or destitute), has become a fertile ground for soldiers (willing or unwilling to fight a war that a great majority of them know nothing about).

Some families in Sudan believe that the only way they can survive is if their sons go to war. Many are left with a most difficult decision to send a child who had just survived a horrific civil war to fight another. In interviews, some of these child fighters who have returned are unable to articulate in words, what they have been through. Those that do, say children make up at least 20-40% of the units. And they are largely fighting alone. The Saudi or

Emirate commanders reportedly keep a safe distance from the warfronts and give instructions almost exclusively via remote-controlled radios. Many of the children have never seen these commanders, or laid eyes on them, but they take their place in what I am calling the *death rollcall*.

Like the Yemenis, many of the Darfurian boys are as young as 8-10 years old and are often recruited under the pretext of assisting their families with financial needs. Saudi Arabia is known to promise families as much as $10,000 to fight in a war that is more than 1200 miles away in Yemen. *"Some families are so eager for the money that they bribe militia officers to let their sons go fight."* UNICEF, the United Nations agency focused on children, which set up a fundraiser for the children of Yemen, here, has verified more than 2,700 cases of children enlisted in combat in Yemen. And depending on the news outlet you read, some have reported up to 50,000 child soldiers (including girls) enlisted in a war where one single enlisted child is one too many.

Eyewitness accounts have reported how these boys are held in unsanitary camps, fed non-nutritious meals, and taught how to use heavy machine guns in a matter of days. They are put to work carrying supplies like food, ammunition, tobacco and *khat* (a narcotic/stimulant alkaloid cathinone which is also often given to the children to keep them awake) to the frontlines. Many of these boys say they don't receive the accurate amounts of money initially promised to them and their family members. But they fight anyway, because any money is *good* money.

Many boys have reportedly run away after only a couple of months in the war front, but sadly many remain, and even sadder, many perish. These children, both those at war and those that are not, have known a very deep and severe trauma, many are living in famine, destitution, and with little or no education and no hope of things getting better any time soon. Posterity will hold us accountable for the lives of these children.

Yemen, an-oil-rich country is now stricken with poverty. It has become what I am calling *the poorest rich country of our time*. Knowing what we know about ACEs, it is nearly of certainty that these children will face a future of the chronic diseases listed above, ***and*** suicide unless rapid and drastic steps are taken to rehabilitate them.

A radically transformative change will be needed. All possible hands must be on deck. We must all sound the alarms and be willing to help in any capacity we can. An immense global campaign must be instituted that is dedicated to ending this crisis against humanity that is largely fueled by selfishness, greed, and a true lack of love for mankind, in order to make a change in the ongoing carnage in Yemen.

UNICEF, along with some independent organizations and non-profit agencies have set up various fundraisers to assist these poor children caught in the middle (see resources page). Support is needed from you and I to help end an ongoing inhumane act that violates human rights and is criminalized by the United Nations (UN).

Chapter 26

STOLEN IDENTITY AND HOPELESSNESS

"The bravest thing I ever did was continuing my life when I wanted to die."

~ Juliette Lewis

Jed'da

Hello Dr. Lulu,

My name is Jed'da which means *"little wild goose."* I am 17. I hail from Thursday Island, one of the nearly 300 islands in the Strait, collectively called the Torres Strait Island communities in Queensland, Australia. I am writing to tell you a little bit about me and my life thus far, I don't know if you can help me or not, but I am willing to give it a try. I was born in a little hut where I live with my parents, my grandmother and my seven brothers and three sisters. All my uncles, aunts and extended family live close by. We, as Indigenous people have always been poor. We have always been oppressed. We have always had a scarcity and lack social services that the rest of the Australian population have. They have systematically taken everything away from us, our language, our art, our names, our dignity and now they want to take away our spirits and our souls.

I was born a free spirit, but I live in a land that threatens to dim my light and sentence it to bondage. I am currently in high school, but public schools here are a land of violence and despair. In my *"neck of the woods,"* the Whites live in one world and the Indigenous live in another. We, the Aborigines are effectively off the White agenda. I live in a land of empty promises and broken covenants. I live in a land where hopelessness has replaced the food that we eat, and despair has replaced the air that we breathe.

After school I often go find my cousin Kalti at the woods and we hang out. We both love to wander and appreciate nature and just talk. He is another free spirit like me. He taught me everything I know about life. He has an infectious laughter, and is generally fun to be with, but his eyes reflect pain, disappointment and dejection. Not unlike most other teens on these Strait Islands. Most of us have lost a will to live, a will to survive. Generations of trauma and abuse have led to sheer disdain and distaste for life and living. And when you have this much hopelessness, alcohol and drugs become everyone's constant companion.

When I was 15, I was raped by my one of my uncles during one of his drunken rages, and nothing was officially done about it. We don't have any social services or police or any form of government assistance. There is no law or order, anything and everything goes. Kalti, was the only one I told about the rape. He was so upset after I told him, that he went on a vengeance fight to beat up my uncle. And they both ended up hurting each other very badly. That was when the news got out and my uncle became the village *"bad soul."* He was ostracized by the community to the point that his alcoholism and drug use worsened.

One night a loud scream and a haunting wail pierced the silence of the night… The sound was not strange to me. That is usually the cry that folks with dying souls make around here. But this time, it was different. The voice was eerily familiar, it was close to home. It was a voice that belonged to my family. I knew it was my uncle even before the news got to us in the morning. He had hung himself on a tree. As is our custom, the tree trunk was cut down and its stump left as a reminder. But how many more trees can we afford to lose? How many more stumps do we need as reminders? What is a life worth around here? Can you answer me, Dr. Lulu?

That was 2 years ago. Since then rapes and sexual assaults of many of the teenage girls have continued. It appears to be the in-thing nowadays. Many people have lost hope and purpose. Because alcohol and drugs are a constant, crime follows them as well. And the government does not appear to be doing anything about it, at least, not that I can see.

Since my cousin and I are such pals, we hang out together a lot. Did I tell you he dropped out of school? Yes, he did, after his promising athletic career was side railed when the government failed to give him the financial support he deserved to help him go further with his career and academics. On some days, when he is not in the woods, I usually find him drinking with other youth, mostly dropouts too, or those who simply never bothered to go to school. Many times, fights breakout amongst them when they run out of liquor. Kalti had his face punched up and bloody one of those times, but the very next day, he returned, and they were pals at the bottle again. Such is the plight of the average Island teen in this part of the world.

Kalti has been having it rough lately. He too has been struggling with alcoholism and a severe case of purposelessness and depression. He has never really recovered from the disappointment concerning his athletic career, at least that was what he said. He always talked about it, about the injustice of it. Unimaginably, just last month, the sound of wailing rang again through one dark starless night. It was long and haunting. I woke up and took off in its direction. I never made it on time. It was Kalti. He had had enough.

These days I spend a lot of time on my own. I go to Kalti's tree stump and sit on it. I think about where he is now. Is he truly free? Should I join him? Could I join him? Would that make me free as well? I doubt that things will ever get better for my people. We are after all, children of the night. We remain invisible. Recently, it was rumored that the Australian government voted to disallow teaching of our culture in the schools. The curriculum does not provide for that anymore. They also just dissolved the Indigenous ruling counsel of the aborigines that was formed in the 1980s, but their reason is that they are trying to *"unify Australia?"* How? The worst thing is that due to gentrification, a lot of the Indigenous communities are no longer able to afford to live on their own land any more. When will it ever stop?

Night draws nigh. I sit here. Looking around. Will anyone listen out for my wail? Will a tree finally set my soul free? Will I find a tree that is worthy to liberate me? Will a tree stump bring comfort to my spirit, or even my family and friends? Will I only then become the (free) wild goose I was born to be?

Jed'da

Dear, dear Wild Goose,

As much as I love the meaning of your name, I can't stop my heart from breaking as I read your letter. I can't begin to imagine the level of despair it takes for the young of the species to lose hope at such an early age. I am steadily shaking my head even as I respond to the letter. I am imagining myself at your age. What would my life had been like if I had been faced with the level of injustice and challenges you and your peers are facing? And to worsen it, the government doesn't seem to be taking any notice, at least from your standpoint.

Tears fill my eyes even as I write this. Will there ever be any respite for you?

Is there any way you and some of the youth who are willing, can get together and start something positive? A youth support group, maybe? You write so eloquently. Would you consider poetry? You could write about your life and struggles. You could perform it for your community. You could even put on a play together. Do it in honor of your cousin, Kalti. I know he won't be there in person, but I bet you he will be front and center in spirit. Do you believe in the spirit of the dead hanging around? I do! So, anything you can do to avoid staying in a rut is better than nothing. The fact that you are reaching out means you are not happy with the way things are going, and that means you are willing to make a change. *"Once there is a will, there is a way."* I believe that quote with all my heart.

In my research, I came across some organizations that seem to have heard your outcry and are doing something about your situation. Could it be that their efforts have not reached your neck of the woods? Please look at the resources portion below and see which of them you could reach out to for some assistance. Let's also look for resources on the internet that could help. Let's organize community-wide activities to empower the youth. Let's continue to push and ask questions, demand answers from your local and regional representatives. And as you get older, who knows, one day you might run for office. Wouldn't it be awesome if you went on to maybe become a lawyer and made the much-needed changes? That would be one way to begin to make a difference in the legal landscape of the land, right?

For now, I would say go home my sweet child. Let's get you home tonight. Leave the trees alone. Let them be. Let your living spirit become free. You have got it within you. You are a ray of light that needs to shine. So, let's get your mind out of that darkness right away, okay?

I will let you go for now. Please know that I am routing for you. Kalti is cheering you on. The youth of Thursday Island are waiting for their heroine... So, go forth and begin to make a difference, today.

Again, thank you so much for reaching out, Wild Goose ☺

Yours in freedom,

Dr. Lulu.

Discussion

"Injustice anywhere is injustice everywhere," Martin Luther King Jr. No wiser words have ever been spoken. That quote rings so true in this situation. Indeed, if one of us is in bondage, then all of us are in bondage. Even the proverbial jailer (warden) must wear a uniform too. By this I mean that systems and governments that refuse to recognize that all humans are created equal, must themselves also suffer the consequences of their shortsightedness and lack of inclusivity.

Apparently, youth suicide in Australian Indigenous tribes is not a new phenomenon. In 2017, it was the leading cause of death amongst children aged 5 to 17, and in 2018, it was actually declared an epidemic. Even though Aboriginal and Torres Strait Islanders account for just 2.8% of the population, over the past five years, one in every four Australian children who died by suicide was Indigenous.

As was mentioned in part one of this book, in January of 2018, there was a suicide cluster involving multiple Indigenous teens over the course of only a few weeks, the youngest of which was only 12. Tragically, a third of youth suicides in the community occur in those who have suffered sexual abuse, and alcoholism and drug abuse only worsen an already dismal situation.

According to some statistics, Indigenous children in Australia die from suicide at five times the rate of their non-Indigenous peers (10·1 per 100 000 vs 2 per 100 000 in 2013–17). This seems to be a recurring pattern in youth of other Indigenous people of settler countries such as New Zealand, Canada and the United States, where struggles to recover from colonization is a very real issue. For instance, similar data are reported in New Zealand, where the suicide rate in Maori youth aged 15–24 years is 40·7 per 100 000 vs 15·6 per 100 000 in non-Maori youth. In Inuit youth in Canada the figure is a staggering 11 times the non-Indigenous average. We already discussed the rates for the Natives Americans and Pacific Islanders of the United states, and the fact that African American youth now have twice the rate of suicide attempts as their White counterparts in the United States. These numbers should tell us something (think generational trauma, think ACEs, think oppression, think racism).

These observations then beg the argument that oppression, systematic racism, and in some cases, dehumanization is the root cause of the rise in suicides in the youth of today. In December of 2018, the Australian senate concluded that the *"primary cause of suicide in Aboriginal and Torres Strait Islander people was not* *mental illness, but dispossession resulting from severe social and* *economic poverty. 60% of Indigenous Australians live below the* *poverty line and 12·5% are homeless."* One study even went as far as stating it clearly, that *despair, not depression* is the cause of the high rates of suicide in their youth.

What is needed is a system that empowers these fragile populations. A system which gives them some autonomy, one which truly frees them. One devoid of childhood traumas as we saw in part one's discussion of ACEs. One which gives them the autonomy and support to seek and fulfil their destinies. They need to have access to proper resources, and an unrestricted ability to figure out the solutions to their unique ethnic-specific problems. If solutions are offered by the government, then the youth must be key participants in every facet of its design and delivery. Their culture must be maintained. We read that Mexican American teens struggle with identity and assimilation into a new culture. The same applies to Australian Indigenes. They must be allowed to have their cultural identity and retain as much of it as possible to maintain their dignity and pride in their heritage.

Lastly, the lack of mental health services suited to individual cultures, poverty, and in the case of the United States, police brutality, racial profiling and overall hostility of the current political climate plays a massive role in the Black youth experience of helplessness. There is an overall lack of trust in the system and a feeling of entrapment. Many Indigenous youth feel they have nowhere to turn for help, and no means to improve their lives, which ultimately fuels the urge to end it all, hence the rise in suicides.

It is imperative that governments improve public health policies and invest in the Indigenous communities. Australia has pledged to spend nearly $4 billion by 2022 to provide culturally appropriate mental health and suicide prevention services for Indigenous people. Two trials of interventions to encourage positive help-seeking behaviors in Indigenous youth are underway. This is such a great start, and if successful, should be emulated and implemented by other governments facing a similar predicament with youth suicides. Any intervention should be introduced in a culturally appropriate way, through Indigenous organizations. They should be sustainable within the population—these trials are rightly co-designed and implemented by Indigenous youth and community leaders. Strategies for poverty eradication, early support for trauma, and recovery programs for substance abuse are urgently needed to address the underlying social determinants that cause these young people's desperation.

Remember this...

In all my years of working with teens and adolescents, one thing that has not changed is the fact that teens are in a transitional world. They are not quite adults and no longer children. They are restless, and experimentative, they seek independence while still needing the nurture that comes from a loving home environment. They are impressionable and creative, and we must never underestimate the power of their determination. If your teen ever approaches you with a problem, the best advice I would give as a parent and as a pediatrician is: listen, be present, be non-judgmental, and be truthful when dealing with them.

The most important thing your teen wants from you is what I like to call *valifreakingdation*. Validation, in the form of acceptance, respect, and allowing them to explore their limits within reason. Don't expect them to grow up to be like you, they will grow up to be like themselves, each into their own person. *Teens don't speak adult, they speak teen*, but you must know and understand their love language in order to fully communicate with them, whether at home or on a larger scale in the community or beyond.

Part 3

Forging Ahead, Finding Solutions, Facing the Future

"When I was experiencing suicidal ideations, the medicines they gave me made me more suicidal"

~ Dr. Lulu

Chapter 27

PUTTING IT ALL TOGETHER

So, what do all these teens have in common? Perhaps you see yourself in one of their stories. Perhaps you know someone going through one of these scenarios at this very moment. Parents, maybe that someone is your child. Young adults, teens and tweens, maybe they are your best friend, your sister, your favorite cousin, or perhaps, it's you.

As we have just read in part 2 of this book, each of these teens represents a group of teens from different parts of the world. Each with a country, region, or ethnic-specific problem. According to the Journal of Adolescent health jahonline.org, teen depression was declared a global health priority in 2013, by the WHO. For a myriad of reasons, especially a lassitude in acknowledging that the problem exists, lack of proper resources for those affected to get help, and most importantly, the stigma associated with a simple mention of the word *depression*, the problem has continued to be on the rise. Mental illness has now become a major burden in adolescent medicine, with depression being on the forefront. Suicide, often associated (accurately or not) with depression, is now one of the leading causes of death in adolescents in all regions of the world. However, this book is not about depression or suicide, it is about the troubles that teens encounter as they transition through life. The decisions some of them have made based on their circumstances and the prices some of them are paying or have paid as a result of it.

According to the National Institute of Health (NIH) adolescence begins with the onset of physiologically normal puberty and ends *when* an adult identity and behavior are accepted. I know, it sounds rather vague, right? My preferred definition is; An adolescent is a person in the *process of developing* from a child into an adult, with the emphasis on *developing*. This period falls roughly between the ages of 10 and 19 years. This definition and age range is also consistent with the World Health Organization's definition of adolescence. It means that adolescent brains are still going through major changes in the transition from childhood to adulthood. In addition, their brains are also highly vulnerable to mood disorders, substance abuse and suicide. We see this vulnerability play out in the lives of all the teens we looked at in this book. This is important because we know that stress or the inability to handle stress can often lead to these outcomes in teens, so, we must be careful not to subject them to much more stress than they often are already placing on themselves.

To date, no intervention for suicidality has been shown to consistently reduce suicide, this is partially because most of you reading this have the same erroneous mindset as that of big pharma, thinking mental illness alone is responsible for suicide deaths. We all know that for effective solution, we need a combination of the right diagnosis and the right treatment. So far, we are falling short on that, so, teen suicide rates continue to soar.

While many of the teens featured in this book did not die by suicide, we have seen that most, if not all of them were in despair. They may or may not have fit the diagnosis of mental illness. However, they are all plagued with anguish and what I call *"overwhelmness"*, these are the ingredients for suicidal behavior.

In 2012, the WHO came forth with a classification for the risk factors for suicide, the three broad classes, (see below) are: individual, sociocultural and situational. Mental illness was only one of the individual factors. My point is, we, as a world must stop focusing on mental illness as the sole cause of suicidal behavior. A closer look at this table will show you a multitude of other reasons that are much more common in the lives of our teens than mental illness.

Chapter 28

SYMPTOMS AND RISK FACTORS

OF SUICIDALITY

INDIVIDUAL	SOCIO-CULTURAL	SITUATIONAL
Mental disorder	Stigmatization of health-seeking behavior	Social losses and breakdown of significant emotional relationships
Alcohol or Drug abuse	Lack of access to healthcare services, including mental health	Financial difficulties
Hopelessness	Cultural and religious beliefs glorifying suicide as a noble outlet in the fact of personal difficulties	Ready access to lethal means

Previous suicide attempt*	Exposure to suicidal behaviors, through the media and the influence of others who have died by suicide	Stressful life events
Isolation and lack of social support		
Aggressive tendencies		
Impulsivity		
History of trauma and abuse (ACEs)		
Acute emotional distress		
Major physical or chronic illness		
Family history of suicide		

Risk factors for suicide, adapted from WHO publication, 2012

Curtesy of Public health action for the prevention of suicide* WHO 2012

*Previous suicide attempt is the greatest risk factor for a suicide death.

In addition to the factors listed above, today's children and teens also have *social media* to deal with. There is a major need to *"roll with the Joneses"* and some of them get too overwhelmed and cave-in to the pressure to conform to the latest hype. Coupled with cyber bullying, and fear of missing out (FOMO), kids these days are subjected to a lot of stress through their handheld devices. On Instagram for instance, children can actually see images glorifying suicide! They are able to easily learn ways to kill themselves. Did you know that? Well, I didn't until recently. Accidental death as a result of risky behaviors, like asphyxiation challenges (as mentioned in part one of this book) is also a common cause of death almost unique to youth. And lastly, LGBTQ+ sexual orientation is a also a huge risk factor for youth suicide, especially Trans youth.

Symptoms of Suicidality

As we noted above in the letters, risk factors for depression, anxiety and other anguish-causing situations can arise from day to day activities and interactions with each other. Adolescents are very impressionable, and often influenced by peer behavior. I chose to highlight different agonizing situations with each teen to showcase the range of stressors they can encounter. As mentioned above, the brain of the teenager is highly vulnerable to extreme emotions, because their brains are still developing. So, teens are oftentimes not capable of fully understanding or navigating their own emotions. They are also unable to fully decipher consequences of their actions. But they deserve to be treated with dignity and respect, regardless of our preconceived notions about them. Suicide involves the interplay of multiple risk factors. Sometimes stressful life circumstances can serve as tipping points and trigger suicidal behavior in adolescents who are already at increased risk.

Chapter 29

IS PATH WARM?

This is a mnemonic that highlights the major symptoms of suicidal behavior. In other words, the signs to look for. Please remember that 4 out of 5 teens who attempt suicide leave signs, so, look for, and try to recognize them if present in your teens. The key thing is to be open minded, ask direct questions and take threats seriously, because *the greatest risk factor for a suicide death is a suicide attempt.*

I stands for Ideation or thoughts, planning, and preparation for suicide. Verbalization, poetry, essays, journaling, saying goodbye, buying a gun, collecting pills, or not taking their meds. Does the person feel or act or even verbalize that they are better off dead? When you ask them the question directly, do they answer *"yes?"* A friend once told me that it is easier for someone to say *"yes"* than to say, *"I need help."* If that is the case, then I suggest we begin to ask all those difficult questions. And be prepared to take them to get help.

S is for Substance abuse, which tends to be present in many cases of hopelessness like we saw in a couple of our teens in part 2. They might suddenly increase their substance use. They often start with alcohol or tobacco and then progress to other substances.

P is for Purposelessness, another common occurrence especially in most of the Indigenous teens highlighted in our stories. They often express a lack of purpose and might see little sense in continuing to live.

A is for Anger. Indeed, many people who feel hopeless also tend to be angry with themselves, with their situations, and with the world in general. They feel like they are unable to control any of the circumstances that are happening to them, and that is understandable. They might also be angry at the persons that they hold responsible for their situations and might become vengeful.

T is for Trapped. Like one blogger described, suicidal people feel like they are backed in a corner, unable to find respite or a way out of their problems. Most feel like this is truly the end of the world and would prefer death to their current predicament. Another blogger described it as jumping out of the window of a high-rise story building to avoid oncoming flames in a burning room. Many have used up all their options and simply lost the will to fight anymore. Most, if not all the teens highlighted in our stories felt trapped.

H is for hopelessness, and I might add, helplessness as well. This is the culmination of the factors we have seen so far. When someone feels hopeless and helpless and feels like they have nowhere else to go, feel unloved, invisible, and unappreciated, it is understandable that they will feel a need to end it all. We must therefore be vigilant, and ensure we are connecting with our teens and children on a granular level. They mostly crave validation and understanding, not control and unrealistic expectations from the adults around them.

W is for Withdrawal. Many suicidal persons become withdrawn. This was the presentation of our teen from India. She found herself trapped and unable to control her destiny. She was doomed to a life of child marriage, with no apparent way out of it. Again, not mental illness, but mental anguish was the cause of her suicide. Ironically, some persons become more outgoing and even extroverted after the decision to suicide has been made. I think the bottom line is being hypervigilant and hyper aware of drastic changes in their behavior. Then acting accordingly and timely.

A is for Anxiety. *"Worriation"* is a term I learned when I lived in the Carolinas. It refers to an extreme state of worrying. This is almost a given when one finds themselves faced with unsurmountable obstacles. Our Native American teen had some anxiety. These symptoms should never be treated as a cry for help. They often are in a state of agitation, with lack of sleep, excessive sleep sometimes and inability to relax.

R is for Recklessness. Teens by nature are often reckless sometimes. However, when a person is suicidal, they can become reckless to the point of not considering or preferring the potential consequences. Like driving fast without a seatbelt, or engaging in promiscuity, or even hitchhiking and or refusing to take the meds needed for their treatments, like our teen from Kenya.

M is for Mood changes. A dramatic change in mood, or excessive moodiness might set in when one is suicidal. There might also be a rapid change in extremes of moods. However, this could also simply be a sign of a mood disorder, so, each symptom must be taken in context. And a specialist must be contacted to evaluate any suggestive behavior.

Chapter 30

MENTAL ANGUISH VS MENTAL ILLNESS
IN TEENS

This book is primarily about teens and the issues they deal with in their day to day lives. Though mental illness is one of them, it is primarily about the mental anguish that results from a culmination of all the *"drama"* they often must deal with. Even when we address mental illness, many parents who have a history of mental illness themselves, still fail to recognize or accept the signs in their children. My first patient that died of suicide, unfortunately, was in that group (see part 1). Besides the teens themselves, their friends and family, schoolmates and other acquaintances must also frequently face the diagnoses with them and should be willing to be supportive. Essentially, the entire community should be involved when a child suffers emotionally.

Mental anguish has also been linked to certain forms of extreme violence, and to some extent, the rise in school shootings in the United

States. Many of the news outlets suggest that mental illness is behind these shootings, but, the kids involved in the Columbine shooting 20 years ago for instance, had been reportedly ostracized and bullied and were essentially outcasts. Although the latest news is refuting that fact, we might never know for sure. The bottom line is that no one wants to be an outcast, especially in school

As a matter of fact, 8 out of 10 kids who call the crisis text line, mention school as a source of their stress or distress, and, 56% of kids who attempt suicide, have been bullied. Supporting the argument in favor of mental anguish.

We all have a primal need to belong to something, somewhere or someone. We all need to feel loved and appreciated and even wanted. We all want to count in some way. However, mental illness has also been recorded as a cause of mass shootings, according to research, at least 59% of the nearly 500 public mass shootings that have taken place in the United States from 1900 through 2018 were carried out by people who had either been diagnosed with a mental disorder or demonstrated signs of serious mental illness prior to the attack. The shooter at the Aurora movie theater in Colorado reportedly did have a history of mental illness. As a matter of fact, my neighbor's daughter was killed in that shooting ☹.

The worst consequence of unrecognized or untreated mental anguish is death through suicide. The death of a child or teenager is extremely difficult as it is, but death through a self-inflicted injury is the absolute worst. It is often unimaginable. In one of the episodes of my podcast, Suicide Pages, I interviewed the author of the book *"Shattered"*, a mother who lost her then 17-year-old son to suicide. According to her, they had no idea why he did it. He had left absolutely no signs that they had noticed prior. However, during the interview, we were able to uncover multiple signs that her son had left but were completely unrecognized by his family, his teachers and even his close friends. His suicide left his grieving family and the entire community in a very difficult place. There were often lots of unanswered questions, lots of guilt, lots of self-blaming, and lots of shaming of his family, according to his mom. True devastation. I am determined with my work, to draw attention to this rising cause of untimely death.

Chapter 31

25 MYTHS ABOUT SUICIDE

Before we embark on what we can all do to prevent suicide in our teens and youth, I think it is only proper to discuss some of the myths about suicide that are floating around. Debunking them will help increase awareness of their falsehood and help fill in the critical knowledge gaps. Here are 25 that I could find, enjoy ☺

- *Suicide is not a real problem in youth*: As we all know, suicide is a real problem in our world today, it is now the second leading cause of death in our youth. Self-destructive behavior is more likely to become manifest in adolescence, so we must be vigilant.

- *Asking your teen about suicide causes suicidal behavior*: Talking about suicide not only increases awareness and puts an end to the shame and stigma, it also helps teens explore other options and keeps open communication lines.

- *The person/family needs more prayers and more Jesus*: While having a sense of belonging to a religious community or spiritual group is always encouraged and actually protective of suicide, it does not in of itself prevent suicide. However many suicidal persons have said that when they reached out for help, they were told they were being dramatic or selfish or needed to pray more.

- *Religious persons do not die by suicide*: Just this past summer we heard about the young American pastor who was active in the mental health arena, who actually lost his life to suicide, there have been many others including a Nigerian pastor as well.

- *Young persons thinking about suicide cannot help themselves*: While contemplating suicide, young people may have a distorted perception of their actual life situation and what solutions are appropriate for them to take. However, with support and constructive assistance from caring and informed people around them, young people can gain full self-direction and self-management in their lives.

- *Only professionals can offer effective interventions for suicide*: All people who interact with adolescents in crisis can help them by way of emotional support and encouragement. Psychotherapeutic interventions also rely heavily on family, and friends providing a network of support.

- *Denial, it does not happen to our ethnicity or family (Blacks, Asians)*: This thought process as we know is erroneous, and Black kids were recently documented as attempting and dying by suicide more and more. Suicide is also high among Asian youth, and pretty much all races and ethnicities.

- *Only a professional can identify a child at risk for suicide*: One of the reasons for this book and my work in the suicide arena is to increase awareness, by educating everyone about the signs, so we are all more empowered. Once we all know what to look for and what to do, the rest should follow through.

- *Once someone is suicidal, they will always be suicidal*: For the most part, suicidal thoughts and behavior are situational and temporary. Most suicidal persons need to know that the feelings can and do pass once they are equipped with the right tools to deal with their thoughts and have the necessary support they need.

- *Only people with mental illness are suicidal*: When I was going through my suicidal stage, I had never been diagnosed with mental illness, I did however experience a lot of life challenges which shook my core and caused me to consider myself a failure and not worthy of living. During the financial crisis of 2008, there was a sharp rise in suicides, up to 10,000 men reportedly died by suicide as a result of the enormous financial losses they had experienced, and not from *prior* mental illness.

- *Most suicides happen suddenly and without warning*: We know that 4 out of 5 teens who attempt suicide leave warning signs. The decision to suicide is hardly ever a one-off thing, it is usually a culmination of events over time leading to what I call *"overwhelmness"* and inability to cope.

- *Someone who is suicidal wants to die*: In all honesty, most suicidal people don't want to die. They simply want their pain and suffering to end. They often feel like they have exhausted all their options and like we mentioned above, they also have a means to end their lives.

- *Someone who is threatening suicide is not going to carry it out*: I like to always say, *"don't underestimate the power of determination."* Because we can never be too sure of what someone will or will not do. ***We must therefore take every suicide threat seriously.*** It should never be assumed to be attention-seeking, and disregarded. Part of the reason suicide is on the rise is also because these people sometimes feel like their issues are belittled, and not taken seriously.

- *If a person is suicidal, there is nothing you can do*: Suicidality like we already mentioned is temporary. You must start by first believing them, then getting them the right kind of support and care, right away.

- *Suicide is hereditary*: Although suicide can be over-represented in families, attempts are not genetically inherited. Members of families share the same emotional environment, and the death by suicide of one family member may well raise the awareness of suicide as an option for other family members.

- *Only certain types of people become suicidal*: Everyone has the potential for suicide, not only those who have mental illness. Sudden acute traumatic life events can also become triggers like bankruptcy, divorce, death of a child, loss of a job, or burnout from work etc.

- *A promise to keep a note unopened and unread should always be kept*: Where the potential for harm, or actual harm, is disclosed then confidentiality cannot be maintained. A sealed note with the request for the note not to be opened is a very strong indicator that something is seriously amiss. A sealed note is a late sign in the progression towards suicide. Please ensure you get the person proper help ASAP.

- *Most suicides happen in the Winter:* Suicide is not just related to the seasons and the climate being hotter or colder, and having more, or less light. It has much more complex etiologies. In general, suicide is more common in the spring, and there's a noticeable peak on New Year's Day.

- *People who talk about suicide will never attempt:* Talking about suicide can be a plea for help and it can be a late sign in the progression towards a suicide attempt. Those who are most at risk will often show other signs apart from talking about suicide. However, a high index of suspicion is important to pick on the subtle signs.

- *Suicide is painless:* Many suicide methods are very painful. Fictional portrayals of suicide do not usually include the reality of the pain. And some people have told me that the fear of incompletion often dissuades them from attempting.

- *Suicide can always be prevented by outsiders:* No matter how well-intentioned alert and diligent people's efforts may be, there is no way of preventing all suicides from occurring. This is an important point for survivors to know. They are often laden with guilt. But in honesty, though the circumstances often are preventable, the act itself can sometimes take place in spite of every appropriate effort being in place.

- *Breakups in relationships happen so frequently, that they don't cause suicide:* Suicide can definitely be precipitated by the loss of a relationship. A breakdown in relationships like a divorce is high on the causal list for suicide.

- *Young people thinking about suicide will be angry if someone tries to help them:* While it is common for young people to be defensive and resist help at first, these behaviors are often barriers imposed to test how much people care and are prepared to help. For most adolescents considering suicide, it is a relief to have someone genuinely care about them and to be able to share the emotional burden of their plight with another person. When questioned sometime later, the vast majority express gratitude for the intervention.

- *People who die by suicide are selfish and taking the easy way out*: Because these people have been suffering for a while, majority of them actually feel like suicide not only puts an end to their suffering, it also frees them from being a burden to others. Many suicide attempt survivors say they feel their lives are a burden to those around them.

- *Sudden improvement in the mental state after a suicide crisis means the risk is over*: In the first three months following an attempt, a young person is at most risk of dying by suicide. The apparent uplifting of moods could mean the person has made a firm decision to die and thus, feels better because of this decision.

Chapter 32

SO, WHO DOES WHAT, AND WHAT TO DO?

The Government

As mentioned elsewhere in this book, suicide in teens and young adults is on the rise. As suicide is a sensitive issue—and even illegal in some countries—many cases go unreported, but suicide is also largely preventable. It is a permanent solution to mostly temporary problems. Most of the governments of the world have not made suicide a global and mandatory issue, and that is a barrier to its prevention. Suicide characteristics differ based on a country's economic status. Because rising deaths by suicide say something about the conditions under which people live and die, and about the society at large, prevention of suicide at any age, must be at the top of everyone's agenda if we are to succeed at it. While people are beginning to take note of the numbers, so far, not much appears to be going on at most governmental levels.

We need to act now to prevent as many potential teen suicides as possible in our communities. Short- and long-term action is essential. Long-term action must begin to address the traumatic, disrupting and intergenerational effects of colonization and its aftermath: poverty and social exclusion. As we have seen highlighted in our teens, these are deep-rooted contributors to suicide in their age group.

The prevalence, characteristics and methods of suicidal behavior vary widely between different communities, in different demographic groups and over time. Consequently, up-to-date surveillance of suicides and suicide attempts is an essential component of national and local suicide prevention efforts. This task is much more difficult than it appears. Obtaining high-quality actionable data is difficult in view of suicides being stigmatized or illegal in many countries. Until countries and communities recognize suicide as a public health danger and provide support to those attempting suicide—we will be losing the fight to prevent suicides.

According to the WHO, governments play a crucial role in this fight. The following text is from their online publication.

- The first step is to create a national strategy, stating a clear commitment to suicide prevention. Currently, only 28 countries have such a strategy. Ensuring collaboration between multiple stakeholders and sectors—public and private—is essential.

- Countries must restrict access to the most common means of suicide, like restricting access to pesticides and rat poison in India and Nigeria respectively. Evidence from Australia, Canada, New Zealand, the United States and several European countries suggests that restricting access to firearms has been associated with a drop in firearm suicide rates.

- Follow-up care by health workers for people who have attempted suicide is critical, as they are at great risk of trying again. Social support within communities can help protect people who are vulnerable to suicide by building their coping skills and sense of connectedness. Communities *must* provide nurturing environments to those who are vulnerable, and governments can set a good example to enable them to do so.

- Responsible media reporting has been shown to decrease suicide rates (contagion and clusters). This includes educating the public about suicide, risk factors and where to seek help, avoiding sensationalism and glamorization, and avoiding detailed descriptions of suicidal acts (I don't completely agree with this point, I believe that we have to state facts in order to accurately gather data, but I do agree that the appropriate information should be given only to those who need it for research.) Governments can help media with these efforts by releasing public service announcements that raise awareness, identifying and treating mental and substance use disorders as early as possible, and ensuring those vulnerable to suicide receive the care they need before it is too late. Mental health and alcohol policies should be integrated into overall health-care services, and governments should ensure adequate funding is provided to improve these services.

- Worldwide, the prevention of suicide has not been adequately addressed due to lack of awareness. And I might add, the lack of acceptance of suicide as a major problem *and* suicide being a taboo in many societies hinders the ability to openly discuss it. In fact, only a few countries have included prevention of suicide among their priorities, and Nigeria, my country of birth is not one of them. As of November 2019, Ghana is in the process of overhauling their national suicide policy which originally criminalized suicide attempts. Suicide prevention requires intervention from all sectors and calls for an innovative, comprehensive, multisectoral approach, including both health and non-health sectors, e.g. education, labor, police, justice, religion, law, politics and the media. Suicide prevention is a cornerstone of WHO's Mental Health Action Plan, adopted by the World Health Assembly in May 2013. The plan calls on countries to reduce their rates of suicide by 10% by 2020.

WHO's new report, *"Suicide prevention: a global public imperative,"* is a call to action to make suicide prevention a higher priority on the global public health agenda. World Suicide Prevention Day observed each year on 10 September is a global opportunity to raise awareness and promote joint action to protect those who are vulnerable to suicide.

The following is the condensed version:

- Campaigns to increase public awareness of suicide as a preventable problem, to develop broad-based support for prevention efforts, and to reduce stigma
- Community development to support creation and implementation of suicide prevention programs
- Improved access of services to suicidal people and their loved ones, and improved service delivery efforts through development of guidelines and linkages
- Media education to improve reporting and portrayals of suicide in the media
- Training for caregivers to improve recognition of at-risk behavior and delivery of effective treatments
- Incorporation of licensing standards for professional caregivers
- Development and promotion of effective clinical and professional practices
- Means restriction initiatives to reduce access to lethal means and methods of self-harm

- Research and evaluation to promote and support research, improve surveillance systems, and evaluate the effectiveness of new or existing suicide prevention interventions

I recently discovered that the city of San Antonio is planning to introduce a *"city-wide trauma awareness program"* based on ACEs, and that brings me so much joy.

Parents

I can honestly say that the biggest issues teens have is their parents not being as supportive as they should. By not believing them, not accepting that they truly have issues, or not thinking that a suicide threat in their teen can actually lead to a suicide death. Most parents and caregivers have what I call the *"not my child"* syndrome, essentially, a denial. Now that we know the warning signs, if you think your child might be suicidal, the most important thing to do is accept and believe the *current* situation.

Don't belittle it! It is nothing to be ashamed of, there should be no denial or freaking out. If you already have a family or personal history of depression or suicidal behavior or suicide, then you know its gravity. Your child is most likely not seeking attention. But even if they are, you must seek out the reason for the recent change in your child's personality. This is not one of those times you want to *"pray"* it away, or worse still, look the other way!

Talk to your teen: Talk to your teen's friends. Talk to everyone that knows your teen. Talk to them, talk to all of them. This is the one time you are NOT allowed to maintain privacy... It *is* a matter of life and death. Be honest, be approachable, be empathetic and understanding, be your child's ultimate cheerleader. Most teenagers feel invisible, and unheard. Some of them simply need someone to talk to. They want to feel listened to, and to feel heard. They need you to leave your door open literarily and figuratively. They need the love and understanding and care of their parents. They need to know you've got their backs. You might need to come straight and ask them plainly if they are thinking of killing themselves. Just do it! **It *is* that serious.** And, NO, talking to someone at risk about suicide does not make them engage in the act, if anything, it makes them know that you care.

Do your homework: learn all you can about teen suicide and the role mental ill-health plays in it. Read about it, ask for help from professionals like teachers, school counselors, your child's doctor, as well as family and friends. Monitor your teens' social media accounts. Many teens learn a lot from their friends and from the world wide web, and the dark web. Some teens have followed instructions they found on social media sites like Instagram and killed themselves.

Look around your child's room for any suspicious items: I once had a kid use his computer cord to attempt to strangle himself. And another used a simple pillowcase. Look for a gun, ropes, knives, razors, a suicide note, suggestive essays, poems, drawings, pills etc. You could even look through their journals if need be. Reading their journals is not invasive if you suspect they might be hiding a behavior that could be deadly. Remember Ms. Alexandra Valoras? Don't keep your pills within reach if they are dangerous. Discard them properly. If you have a gun, empty the canister and store it appropriately. Does your child have rope marks on their necks? Cuts on their thighs, arms, legs etc. These may be signs they are engaging in self-harming behavior.

Access the healthcare system: Go to a psychologist or call your child's doctor and set up appointments for your child. Look into all available options for psychotherapy and counseling, and if need be, your child might be institutionalized. Don't be afraid of medications. If diagnosed with mental ill-health, most doctors will titrate your child's meds as tolerated and as necessary to keep symptoms and side effects controlled. Ensure you cooperate fully with your child's doctor. Be honest with their true symptoms.

Healthcare Providers; Clinicians, Doctors, Others

If you are reading this book, then hopefully you have heard, or you know that exactly 1.1 physicians die by suicide each day. That is because the current number is 400 physician suicides per year. And that does not include resident physicians or medical students, many of whom happen to fall in the category of youth or young adults. This was a real hard truth for me, not only because I myself have dealt with suicidal ideations, but also because in the past 12 months, I have lost a total of 5 colleagues to suicide! Unfortunately, physicians do not have much luck when it comes to crying for help, because of a myriad of factors that block the path to getting appropriate care when we do cry.

For these reasons, it is extremely imperative that we as physicians know exactly what to look for in our patients, and what to do if and when we suspect them to be suicidal. Our primary responsibility is to be open-minded and clear-headed when seeing patients. Reports have shown that about half of the patients who have mental illness and subsequently die by suicide were seen by their provider within one month prior to their death.

Our first order of business is to know the facts, know their symptoms, and the risk factors of suicidality in our patients. Ensure that we are able to separate mental health issues from emotional health issues and handle each problem differently, so we don't inadvertently worsen the stigma by piling both issues together. We must let go of any and all intrinsic biases, erroneous thought processes and assumptions when it comes to suicide. Our patients are depending on us. We must in turn do the same for ourselves and for our colleagues.

We must ask the tough questions:

- Am I doing enough?
- Am I aware of ACEs and the role they play in the suicide narrative?
- Do I administer ACEs questionnaires to all my patients with behavioral issues?
- Do I provide adequate counseling and education to the parents, especially if they are responsible in part or in whole for the child's suicidal behavior?
- Am I following the recommended processes and procedures for Assessment, Intervention and Monitoring (AIM) when it comes to suicide?
- Am I doing a thorough follow up on all my cases?
- Do I realize that a prior suicide attempt is the strongest risk factor for a suicide death?
- Am I willing to do whatever it takes to ensure my patient feels loved, supported and cared for?

Most teens find it hard to open up to anyone about their struggles, so we must be sensitive to their needs and show love, empathy and certainly a good dose of compassion when dealing with them. Absolutely no judgement. We need full on mindfulness. The last thing you want is for your patient to shut down and not communicate anymore.

The state of California has now begun a state-wide screening for ACEs in school children, especially those children diagnosed with behavior disorders like ADHD, mental illness, and learning disabilities, thanks to the recommendations of Dr. Nadine Burke. Results of the screening will be discussed with the school and recommendations made to the school district or individual schools to that effect. This is such a great move and I can't wait for it to become standardized across all states.

Educators: Teachers, Counselors, Coaches etc.

Since children and teens spend a lot of time in school, a majority of their stressors like bullying do often arise in school or school-related areas like the school bus or playground. And because there have been many reports of suicides that have occurred in school aged kids, teachers and other educators are at a great advantage when it comes to detecting suicidal behavior and making the appropriate referrals. They can notice what students say, do, or write, and take appropriate action when they suspect a student may be at risk of self-harm. With the current rate of suicides in youth, it goes without saying that teachers must play a huge role in suicide prevention.

The most obvious requirement is awareness. The American Foundation for Suicide Prevention (AFSP) recommends that state governments require a mandatory suicide prevention training for teachers and other school personnel who interact regularly with students, so that they may assist vulnerable youth in accessing the services they need. The schools themselves must also have polices in place for prevention: early detection, intervention and postvention of suicide in their schools. I had no idea about this, especially because most youth suicide reports that result from bullying, often site the school system as *"not having done anything"* to stop the bullying before the suicide occurred.

Teachers can also play an active role by fostering the emotional well-being of all students, not just those at high risk. Risk is greater however in youth who have attempted suicide in the past, lost a close friend to suicide, or one who gets an acute stressful life event (like a parental death or divorce) with or without other preexisting risk factors. Risk is also greater if the warning sign is a new behavior for the student, or a behavior that has increased and could be related to an actual painful event or loss. Like a parental death, sibling death, suicide loss, or substance abuse.

Teachers must have access to the proper referral information and know when and why they must refer the students to the appropriate authority. They must make it a priority to discuss any new symptoms they notice in students with other teachers, the health care team, as well as the student's parents. I would also suggest that ACEs training in schools, communities and civic organizations become a requirement.

The school must ensure:

- Student supervision by an adult at all times. The teen may need someone to walk them to the restroom and keep an eye on them during recess.

- Safe drop off and pick up from school by a designated caregiver.

- No access to potentially harmful substances or instruments including cleaning solutions, sharp scissors or knives, gardening or carpentry tools. In case the student needs to use these substances, they should be closely supervised.

- Provide activities that are pleasurable or enjoyable and encourage the student's participation.

- Be encouraging and supportive, studies have shown that teens who have as many as *only one* adult in their life who cares about them do not harm themselves.

- Encourage the student to have *"ownership"* of something – like taking care of a plant, a classroom pet, or participating in a fundraising campaign.

- Engage the student in long term classroom projects so that they will always have something to look forward to the next day.

- Provide situations where the student can build lasting relationships with other classmates, healthy relationships are known to be protective.

Teens

TALK to someone. **Talk** to someone. *Talk to someone!* Did I already say TALK to someone? The suicide hotline is 1-273-TALK (8255) with emphasis on the word, **talk.** And if you would rather prefer to text, then, the crisis text line is available in the US, in Canada and in the UK (see info in resource section below). HOPELINE is another text service for crisis counseling available in the US. Much like the crisis text line, all you have to do is text the word HOPELINE to 741741 in the US. A live, trained specialist receives the text and responds right away. You can text about *anything, at any time, and from anywhere.* Help is literally only a text away 😊.

In Nigeria, the award-winning Mentally Aware Nigeria Initiative (MANI) is one association that caters to confidential counseling. Whatever part of the world you find yourself, a simple google search will yield a crisis hotline, most of which are confidential, and are there to help. Please KNOW that you are NOT alone. There is a whole world of friends and neighbors and family who love you and want to protect and help you.

Be kind to yourself. Don't allow negative thoughts creep into your head. And if they do, don't let them get comfortable and stay. Practice self-compassion as often as possible and know that your brain likes to tell lies and wants you to be miserable and hurt yourself. Allow friends and family members to help you. A good therapist or clinician can also help you if you would rather speak to a neutral ear. Practice self-forgiveness and self-love. I know this is thrown around a lot these days, but studies have shown that self-compassion can be protective of suicidal behavior.

Don't stay alone if you are suicidal. I would suggest that you not only physically remove yourself from the environment, especially if it there are dangerous means to hurt yourself, but also remove yourself from the thought process that leads you to feel a need to hurt yourself. Reach out. Say something. Get help! Being around people makes a huge difference in the way you perceive situations and affects the thoughts that come into your head. However, be very careful who you ask for help, ensure it is someone who cares enough about you to want to help you. Not everyone is necessarily good for you when you are at a bad place. Only stay around good friends who support and love you. Find family members or mentors or call the suicide hotline. If you have a trusted doctor or counselor reach out to them. If you have the NOT OK app installed on your phone, use it. Ask your parents to set it up for the rest of your family members as well.

Pick up a new hobby. Try playing a musical instrument, gardening, knitting, quilting or journaling. I have a patient who had never drawn anything in her life before, she recently picked up a sketch book and has not looked back, and she is actually pretty good at it. You never know until you try. Learn the new hobby for the first time when you are at an emotionally good place, that way, when you start feeling bad, it will help improve your mood. Most people who get suicidal often say the feeling is temporary, but I also understand how overwhelming that urge can be when you truly think and believe there is no other way out, at that moment.

Get a job. You would be amazed how much your mindset will change once you have a place to go every morning when you wake up. Unless of course the cause of your stress is at work. Getting a job gives you a sense of purpose. It helps you feel like you are needed. It gives you something to distract you and helps you feel connected to something productive. If you are a student and are being bullied at work, then make sure the supervisor and your parents are all aware. That situation should be dealt with right away, and perpetrators should be disallowed from having any kind of contact with you.

Volunteer. *"Life is so much better when you volunteer."* Dr. Lulu. Do you know that volunteering can sometimes be more fulfilling for some than their paying jobs? I believe it is because, when you volunteer, you are giving of yourself without any monetary returns. The emotional returns completely outweigh any afterthoughts about the time you give. You can volunteer at places like Habitat for Humanity, The Ronald McDonald House, orphanages, soup kitchens, Meals on Wheels, or animal shelters to name a few. A quick google search will pull up a lot of places you can volunteer near you. The best part is, many of these places give you service hours as well, so it's a win-win ☺.

Journal. Journaling is such a cool thing to do. You can pour your heart out to your journal. No judgement, no need to try to impress anyone. Your journal is your own private space. No one has to come in there. You can write whatever you like, or don't like. You can rip it up afterwards or save it, either way, you are able to write down your thoughts. The benefits of journaling have been extensively researched and published. You can come up with themes of what to write, you can make it a daily gratitude journal. While you can technically write whatever you like, if you find that you are mostly writing dark stuff, then you might need to reach out to someone. Don't forget to do it daily!

Meditate. Meditation and the practice of mindfulness is one of the guiding principles I teach in my first book, "How to Raise Well Rounded Children," available on Amazon. This practice helps to center your mind, body and spirit. It teaches you to be deliberate and intentional in everything you do. It teaches you to be self-aware and non-judgmental to self. It enables you to practice thinking before acting. Weighing all the options before making a decision. It makes you think about things before you do them and weigh the impact of your words before you say them either to yourself or to others. Overall, mindfulness and meditation help you become more in tune with your senses, your body and your soul.

A YouTube search will yield many sites that help with guided meditations.

Learn the practice of Yoga. This not only helps build muscle strength and flexibility, it also builds inner strength and focus. It helps to cultivate mindfulness (I recommend a book called *"the mindful teen"* by Dzung X. Vo, an adolescent pediatrician). Yoga practice also helps you learn how to control your thoughts, gather them together, bring them to a positive place. It also teaches intentional *ooji* breathing which also helps with your overall psyche.

So, if all else fails, try the following 😊

Get off your cellphone

Tune off social media

Reduce your overall screen time

Get outdoors and take a walk

Read a good book

Plant a garden

Exercise

Phone a friend, not text

Get a pet

Help out around the house

Rinse, and Repeat 😊

Treatment Options

*A combination of medication management counseling is recommended by the American Academy of Pediatrics (AAP), for diagnosed mental illnesses like depression and anxiety.

*Counseling or psychotherapy could be in the form of group therapy sessions, family therapy sessions or individual therapy sessions. They are all effective modalities of treatment often tailored to your specific need as determined by your healthcare team.

*If your situation is grave, your doctor might recommend you be institutionalized. Remember this is often for your own good and cooperate with your caregivers.

Most importantly: Call your doctor, your school counselor, or your therapist. If you or anyone you know is contemplating suicide, CALL 800-SUICIDE, or 800-273-TALK.

Everyone Else

For the rest of the village that it takes to raise and save our children, we all need to be more compassionate, more vigilant and more loving and kinder to one another. Words do matter.

Having the right mind-set and right attitude towards mental illness, and suicide is a huge deal. It helps those who are walking the walk feel a tad bit more secure, more loved and less hopeless. Using the proper verbiage for instance is so important:

AVOID	SAY
Committed Suicide	Suicided
Successful Attempt	Died of Suicide
Failed Attempt	Suicide Attempt
Completed Suicide	Suicide Death
Dramatic/Manipulative/	Describe the behavior
Cry for Help	

Not over sensationalizing it is as important as not talking about it at all. Talking about suicide and being compassionate helps suicidal persons overcome the shame and the stigma involved.

Realizing that majority of suicide deaths are not as a result of mental illness, but rather mental anguish is also key. Knowing the signs and symptoms of suicidality, helping victims get appropriate help, knowing what to say and what not to say are all equally important. Checking in on one another, especially those who appear *"strong and together"* is very critical. And when someone shares their pain with you, don't trivialize it. In the end, we all need to be each other's keepers and have one another's backs, and together we shall create a kinder world free of suicide.

One last suggestion that might work is if all of us gatekeepers: teachers, parents, family members, healthcare providers, clergy, volunteers, coworkers, supervisors, even friends and colleagues could learn QPR. QPR stands for ***"Question, Persuade, Refer"***. It is used particularly to intervene in suicide prevention. Much like CPR, it is designed to teach both professionals and lay persons how to offer hope and take action when they are concerned that someone may be at risk for suicide.

Without going into too much detail, QPR essentially involves a three-pronged approach:

> *Direct questioning like "Are you thinking about suicide or wanting to kill yourself?" Remember that asking the question or talking about suicide does not increase chances of suicide, rather, it helps our friends know that we care and want to help. So, if you suspect something, ask, just ask, you might be saving a life... How cool is would that be?

> *Persuading the person to allow you assist them in getting help *right now*. Like *"Will you go with me to get you help?"* *"Or will you let me help you?"* And if persuasion does not work, then you must call the emergency number, a crisis hotline or a crisis text line (see resources page below).

*Refer the individual to an appropriate source for assistance, or preferably, accompany them on the trip, and then ensure you keep communication lines open and follow up with them. As much as possible avoid simply giving them the information and asking them to follow through by themselves.

Remember that a suicide attempt is the strongest risk factor for a suicide death, so, we want to prevent our friends and loved ones from attempting suicide by all means... I can't stress that enough.

Postvention

Suicide postvention is defined as *"the response to and care for individuals affected, in the aftermath of a suicide attempt or suicide death"* (U.S. Department of Health and Human Services (HHS) Office of the Surgeon General and National Action Alliance for Suicide Prevention, 2010, p. 141). According to the DHHS, the goals of postvention may include:

1) supporting the bereaved survivors with appropriate behavior health services.

2) preventing imitative suicides by identifying other individuals at risk for self-destructive behavior and connecting them to intervention services.

3) reducing survivor identification with the deceased.

4) providing long-term surveillance for individuals and communities at large.

In 1968 Shneidman used the term postvention to describe the interventions deployed to address the bereaved survivors, health care providers, and caregivers of a suicide victim. Its primary aim is to destigmatize suicide, assist in the recovery process and to also serve as secondary prevention against a suicide contagion and possible suicide cluster.

I once read somewhere that every youth suicide affects up to 3000 people. While I can't confirm that number, I do think that-that is very possible, if one includes classmates, neighbors, family members and acquaintances of the deceased *and* their friends and contacts. And if you include social media and virtual friends and communities, then that number can become exponentially much higher. I know for example, that every time a kid dies by suicide, someone usually tags me on Facebook, and whenever I create a post about a child's suicide it usually results in many comments and shares.

Ensuring children and young people exposed to family and community suicide receive postvention support cannot be over-emphasized. It is critical to preventing further suicides in these at-risk youth. The communities that experience youth suicide must ensure that at-risk and vulnerable youth receive a coordinated and timely response, including education, assessment, treatment, follow-up and caring support. School systems are an integral part of a community. As many young people who die by suicide are part of a school community, the school becomes a natural place for a postvention response. In the aftermath of suicide, close attention should be paid to the unique cultural meaning of suicide in that community, as well as to local healing practices for the family, community, and cultural group who have experienced the loss.

Finally, as a practicing pediatrician who has had multiple personal and professional experiences with suicide, including that of my patient, I must add that following the suicide death of a patient, caregivers themselves are survivors and need to have postvention services administered to them. I never had any postvention services, but, my current work was born out of my

259

loss, and my hunger to do something about it. So, I am doing my own part, what about you? What will you do? How will you contribute in making this world a safer place for our youth, and what will you do specifically to make this world, our global village, a suicide-free zone?

Indeed, *"it takes a (global) village to raise a child, and it also takes one to save a child"*.

So, let's go forth!

Namaste ☺
Dr. Lulu®

Poems

<u>Bullying</u>

Do you see me?
Do you know me??

When you call me names?
And pull at my hair
Drag my backpack
And mess up my books
Do you see me?

When you push me and punch me?
And tell tall tales about me
When you jeer each time, I pass by
Do you see my tears?

When my head pounds and my heart aches
My pulse races and my hands sweat
At the thought of waking up...
...to another school day,
Do you even care?

When my back hurts and my stomach cramps
My lips swell and my shins sting
And both eyes are black
From your punches and kicks
Do you feel my pain?

When I cry alone in my room
And refuse mom's best meals,
When I cut my wrists and cut my thighs...
...in tiny slits by day and by night
So as not to feel the hurt you cause
Do you know that?

261

Have you known a pain so deep
From being left out and all alone
When y'all don't look at me, play with me or even speak to me,
When y'all sneer at me and make fun of me,
Do you know what that's like?

Did you know that my *stomaches* never go away?
My leg pains don't get better
My sadness has led to depression
And now I want out?

Al have you know that
I won't tell anyone,
I can't tell anyone because
They don't really care,
They don't want to help
And they can't really help.

I want to end it all

Do you know that I have thoughts?
Thoughts about killing myself,
Thoughts I'd be better off dead
Thoughts about getting a gun
Thoughts about using a knife?

I also have other thoughts
Thoughts about getting even
Thoughts about ending *your* life
Thoughts about getting it done
Ending your lives and mine

Do you know that
When you tease me daily
When you mock me and make me feel small...
...invisible and insignificant
I want badly to get even?

Do you know I have a plan?
I want to show you that
I AM strong
I COULD hurt you
I CAN bounce back
And I WOULD hurt you
Like YOU hurt me.

Yes, I want to hurt you,
AND ensure you are not here when I am done
You will have a hole in your heart,
You will hurt, like I hurt
You will pay for all my pain
Yes, that's my plan.

But you know, don't you?
That I will NOT carry out my plan
That I will NOT hurt you back.

But, one thing is for certain,
I will NOT let you hurt me again, EVER!
I will put an end to it

I will…
…today

To all those who have ever been hurt by bullying, I see you.

Dr. Lulu®

Depression and Suicide

Be the One to…

Speak up

Say something

Ask for help

Reach out

Say I need help

Say I am not doing ok

It's not ok to stay that way

Will you be the one to…?

Look into my eyes and see my pain and anguish?

Know when I am sad and reach out to me?

Know I am depressed and offer a kind word?

Ask me if I am doing ok?

Ask me if I am thinking of hurting myself?

Have the tough conversations with me?

Know that talking to me about suicide will not make me suicidal

Could you please…

Validate my feelings and emotions

Respect my space

Know that I still love you even when I simply want to be left
alone
Not leave me alone when I am sad and needing help
Take me by the hand and tell me it is all going to be ok?

Will you say…

I see you. I know you. I hear you
I am here for you, take my hand
I will take care of you
I will stay here with you
I am here for you.

Will you follow up with me?

When I am being bullied
When I am suicidal
When I am in a bad place?

Sometimes it could be that

I am being bullied
I am being sexually exploited
I am a victim of domestic abuse
I am a victim of divorce or abandonment
I am a victim of emotional or physical abuse

OR

I have a family history of incarceration

I have a family history of mental illness

I have a family history of suicide

I have a family history of substance abuse

Yes, I might be a victim of ACEs

Please know that:

I can still be suicidal even if I don't have mental health issues

I can be suicidal because my friend just died by suicide

Many people who are suicidal don't have mental health
diagnoses

Those who do, do not mainly die from suicide

But if they don't take their meds

Or if they don't have support

Or they experience a recent major trauma

Then they can.

In the past few years,

Prescription antidepressants have quadrupled

Yet suicide rates have continued to rise.

Have you asked yourself why?

Please step out of that line of thinking

That it always boils down to mental health

Because sometimes, it simply isn't.

Dr. Lulu®

RESOURCES

1. Mentally Aware Nigeria Initiative (MANI)
   - www.mentallyaware.org
   - Contact@mentallyaware.org
   - Tel +234-805-149-3163
   - 70, Olonode St, Off Alagomeji, Yaba, Lagos
2. Befrienders Kenya
   - www.befrienderskenya.org
   - befrienderskenya@gmail.com
   - Tel +254-722-178-177
   - La Colline Gardens, Masaba Rd, Off Bunyala Rd,

   Plot No.10, Flat 12

   P.O Box 8660-00100

   Nairobi, Kenya
3. Feeling Kinda Blue
   - www.feelingkindablue.org
4. Self-Harm or NSSI help
   - 1800 DONTCUT or 1-800-366-8288
5. Sexual Assault Help
   - 800.656.HOPE and online.rainn.org

6. National Drug Abuse Hotline: Substance Abuse and Mental Health Services Administration (SAMHSA.gov)
   - 1-800-662-HELP (4357)
   - www.samhsa.gov/find-help/national-helpline
7. Bullying Help
   - Stopbullying.gov
   - https://www.stopbullying.gov/
8. Dr. Lulu's Info
   - www.wordsbyblackbutterfly.com
   - www.teenalive.com
   - www.youthhealthcenter.com
   - (802) - 768 – 1180
9. LGBTQ+ Info
   - The Trevor Project
   - True Colors United
   - The Human Rights Campaign
   - Trans Lifeline (877) 565-8860.
     - Synchronicity Counseling: www.synchronicity-counseling.com
       - 210-853-0503
10. Teen Pregnancy
    - Pregnancylovetoknow.com
    - Planned Parenthood

- Birthright International
- Adoption.com
- Medicaid.gov
- WIC
- YWCA

11. Yemen Help

- International Rescue Committee
- Penny Appeal USA
- The New York Times Fundraiser
- Mwatana For Human Rights
- UNICEF

12. Relaxation and Breathing Techniques

- Breath2Relax app
- 4-7-8 Meditation

13. Indigenous Youth Help

- Indigenous Youth Wellness / email: cuystwi@phsa.ca
- Australian Institute of Family Services: https://aifs.gov.au/

14. Suicide Awareness / Prevention

- Suicide.gov
- 1-800-SUICIDE
- Crisis Text Line

Text HOME to

- US: 741741
- UK: 85258
- Canada: 686868

- The NOT OK app

15. Volunteer opportunities

- Habitat for Humanity Habitat.org
- The Humane Society Humanesociety.org
- Ronald McDonald House Rmhc.org
- Meals on Wheels
  Mealsonwheelsamerica.gov

16. Dr. Lulu's Podcast

- Suicide Pages with Dr. Lulu
- Facebook Groups/Pages

    - Teen Alive
    - Dr. Lulu's Parenting Your Teen
    - Ask Doctor Lulu
    - Suicide Pages
    - Dr. Lulu's Youth Health Center

Appendix 1

Adverse Childhood Experience (ACE) Questionnaire
Finding your ACE Score ra hbr 10 24 06

While you were growing up, during your first 18 years of life:

1. Did a parent or other adult in the household **often** ...
   Swear at you, insult you, put you down, or humiliate you?
   or
   Act in a way that made you afraid that you might be physically hurt?
   Yes No   If yes enter 1   ....

2. Did a parent or other adult in the household **often** ...
   Push, grab, slap, or throw something at you?
   or
   Ever hit you so hard that you had marks or were injured?
   Yes No   If yes enter 1   ....

3. Did an adult or person at least 5 years older than you **ever**...
   Touch or fondle you or have you touch their body in a sexual way?
   or
   Try to or actually have oral, anal, or vaginal sex with you?
   Yes No   If yes enter 1   ....

4. Did you **often** feel that ...
   No one in your family loved you or thought you were important or special?
   or
   Your family didn't look out for each other, feel close to each other, or support each other?
   Yes No   If yes enter 1   ....

5. Did you **often** feel that ...
   You didn't have enough to eat, had to wear dirty clothes, and had no one to protect you?
   or
   Your parents were too drunk or high to take care of you or take you to the doctor if you needed it?
   Yes No   If yes enter 1   ....

6. Were your parents **ever** separated or divorced?
   Yes No   If yes enter 1   ....

7. Was your mother or stepmother:
   Often pushed, grabbed, slapped, or had something thrown at her?
   or
   Sometimes or often kicked, bitten, hit with a fist, or hit with something hard?
   or
   Ever repeatedly hit over at least a few minutes or threatened with a gun or knife?
   Yes No   If yes enter 1   ....

8. Did you live with anyone who was a problem drinker or alcoholic or who used street drugs?
   Yes No   If yes enter 1   ....

9. Was a household member depressed or mentally ill or did a household member attempt suicide?
   Yes No   If yes enter 1   ....

10. Did a household member go to prison?
    Yes No   If yes enter 1   ....

Now add up your "Yes" answers: .... **This is your ACE Score**

Get Your ACE Score ABOVE. Score and tally the numbers to determine your risk for certain diseases and suicidality.

272

References

1. The Parent Resource Program: http://prp.jasonfoundation.com/

2. The Psychiatry Advisor: https://www.psychiatryadvisor.com/depression-advisor/adults-mdd-epidemiology-us-dsm-5/article/750200/

3. Mental Health America: http://www.mentalhealthamerica.net/issues/2017-state-mental-health-america-youth-data

4. The Guardian: https://www.theguardian.com/world/2015/jun/14/chinese-police-investigating-deaths-of-left-behind-children-find-suicide-note

5. The Brooke Haven Retreat http://www.brookhavenretreat.org/

6. The Journal of Adolescent Health: https://www.jahonline.org/article/S1054-139X(13)00122-5/pdf

7. The Boston Globe: https://www.bostonglobe.com/lifestyle/health-wellness/2014/03/09/brain-development-makes-teens-more-vulnerable-suicide-and-mood-disorders/tGBStHOnjqAyanfCe7rbsK/story.html

8. LA Times http://www.latimes.com/opinion/op-ed/la-oe-duwe-rocque-mass-shootings-mental-illness-20180223-story.html"

9. JAMA Network
https://jamanetwork.com/searchresults?q=youth%20nominated%20support%20team&allJournals=1&SearchSourceType=1&exPrm_qqq={!payloadDisMaxQParser%20pf=Tags%20qf=Tags^0.0000001%20payloadFields=Tags%20bf=}%22youth%20nominated%20support%20team%22&exPrm_hl.q=youth%20nominated%20support%20team

10. The Mayo Clinic https://www.mayoclinic.org/diseases-conditions/self-injury/diagnosis-treatment/drc-20350956

Eating disorders
11. Psychology Today https://www.psychologytoday.com/us/blog/minority-report/201706/eating-disorders-spread-among-asians

12. Seattle PI: https://www.seattlepi.com/lifestyle/article/Asian-Americans-and-eating-disorders-A-silent-1106134.php
Kenyan

13. Avert.org: https://www.avert.org/professionals/hiv-around-world/sub-saharan-africa/overview#Barriers%20to%20HIV%20prevention%20in%20East%20and%20Southern%20Africa

14. PLOS.org: https://journals.plos.org/plosone/article?id=10.1371/journal.pone.0190423

15. The United Nations: https://www.un.org/africarenewal/magazine/january-2006/progress-zimbabwe%E2%80%99s-hivaids-battle

Teen Pregnancy
16. CDC.gov: https://www.cdc.gov/teenpregnancy/about/index.htm

17. Americanpregnancy.org: https://americanpregnancy.org/unplanned-pregnancy/teen-pregnancy-issues-challenges/

18. Womenshealth.gov: https://www.womenshealth.gov/30-achievements/09

19. All4kids.com: https://www.all4kids.org/2018/06/07/a-fathers-impact-on-child-development/

Indian
20. Livemint.com: https://www.livemint.com/Politics/YCw8vC0qZUzAYkWSEVXS9N/Suicides-in-India-What-data-shows.html

21. Academy of Pelvic Health: https://www.womenshealthapta.org/blog/vesicovaginal-fistula-in-nigeria/

22. ABC News: https://www.abc.net.au/news/2018-12-02/young-women-india-dying-suicide-alarming-numbers/10562076

Native Americans/Alaskan Indians
23. SAMHSA.gov: https://store.samhsa.gov/system/files/sma17-5050.pdf

24. SAMHSA: https://store.samhsa.gov/system/files/sma16-4969.pdf

275

Nigerian

25. The Guardian: https://www.theguardian.com/commentisfree/2015/sep/09/being-gay-african-history-homosexuality-christianity

26. The Washington Post: https://www.washingtonpost.com/world/47-nigerian-men-plead-not-guilty-to-same-sex-displays-of-   affection/2019/11/28/a604b436-11e0-11ea-924c-b34d09bbc948_story.html

27. The Guardian: https://www.theguardian.com/world/2014/jan/13/nigerian-president-signs-anti-gay-law

Yemen
28. Arab News: https://www.arabnews.com/node/1362296/saudi-arabia

29. The NY Times: https://www.nytimes.com/2018/12/28/world/africa/saudi-sudan-yemen-child-fighters.html

30. Aljazeera.com: https://www.aljazeera.com/news/middleeast/2019/03/exclusive-yemeni-child-soldiers-recruited-saudi-uae-coalition-190329132329547.html

Australian
31. Research Gate:
https://www.researchgate.net/publication/228465754_Aboriginal_language_knowledge_and_yout h_suicide_Cognitive_Development_22_393-399

32. The Lancet: https://www.thelancet.com/journals/lanchi/article/PIIS2352-4642(19)30034-3/fulltext

33. The Guardian: https://www.theguardian.com/australia-news/2019/mar/22/indigenous-suicide-35-dead-in-three-months-including-three-12-year-old-children

34. Theconversation.com: http://theconversation.com/why-are-we-losing-so-many-indigenous-children-to-suicide-114284

Absent Father Syndrome
35. Theroot.com: https://www.theroot.com/the-impact-of-absent-fathers-on-the-mental-health-of-bl-1790853902

36. Wehavekids.com: https://wehavekids.com/family-relationships/When-Daddy-Dont-Love-Their-Daughters-What-Happens-to-Women-Whose-Fathers-Werent-There-for-Them

37. Psychology Today: https://www.psychologytoday.com/us/blog/co-parenting-after-divorce/201205/father-absence-father-deficit-father-hunger

About the Author

Dr. Umeh, AKA Dr. Lulu *"The Momatrician,"* is a National and International Keynote Speaker on Bullying, and Youth Suicide. She is also a Suicide, and LGBTQ+ Activist. She is an Indie Author and Indie Publisher. Her first self-published book *"How to Raise Well-Rounded Children,"* debuted at number one on Amazon's Hot New Releases in the Parenting genre. It is available on her website www.teenalive.com, and on Amazon, in paperback and e-version, and in the Texas Indie library. It received a 5 Star Rating from the Readers Favorites independent review. She is also a freelance writer and frequent contributor to online as well as paper publications, including: Kevinmd.com, Doximity, The Black Parenting magazine, The San Antonio Medicine magazine, and her personal blog www.wordsbyblackbutterfly.com.

Dr. Lulu is on most social media platforms: Facebook and IG as *"ask doctor lulu,"* and Twitter and LinkedIn *as UchennaUmeh9* and *Uchenna L. Umeh* respectively.

She is a wife and a mother of three sons. She lives in San Antonio Texas where she practices medicine seeing only at-risk youth at her direct primary care practice: Dr. Lulu's Youth Health Center (www.youthhealthcenter.com).

Readers can visit her website www.teenalive.com for resources for troubled teens, to book her for speaking engagements, and to sign up for her monthly newsletter.

Made in the USA
Columbia, SC
29 November 2020

25511467R00163